JESSE JAMES
United States Senator

The evidence that
Jesse James
lived to be
103 years of age

by
A. Ralph Epperson

copy right
2005

JESSE JAMES
United States
Senator

published by
PUBLIUS PRESS
3100 South Philamena Place
Tucson, Arizona 85730
the united States of America
telephone (520) 886 - 4380

International Standard Book Number
0 - 9614135 - 5 - 7

Printed in the united States of America

WRITE OR CALL THE PUBLISHER
for a catalog of other books and videos
written and produced by
Ralph Epperson
including his other books
THE UNSEEN HAND;
THE NEW WORLD ORDER;
and
MASONRY
CONSPIRACY AGAINST CHRISTIANITY

DEDICATION

I would like to dedicate
this book to
BUD
HARDCASTLE
the inspiration
to all of us
who are seeking
the truth
about
JESSE JAMES

TABLE OF CONTENTS

TABLE OF CONTENTS
continued

"The history of the War Between the States [the American Civil War, 1861 - 1865] has never been written and the history of the Old West hasn't even been told."

Jesse James
33rd Degree Mason
1948
quoted on p. 7
Jesse James Was One Of
His Names

"Beneath the broad tide of human history, there flow the stealthy undercurrents of the secret societies, which frequently determine in the depths the changes that take place upon the surface."

Arthur Edward Waite
33rd Degree Mason
THE REAL HISTORY OF THE ROSICRUCIANS
page A

". . . the hidden life in Freemasonry [also called Masonry or the Masons] -- the mighty force in the background, always at work yet always out of sight."

Charles Leadbeater
33rd Degree Mason
FREEMASONRY AND ITS
ANCIENT MYSTIC RITES
page ix

". . . the ancient initiates [whom the Masons link themselves to] . . . are the invisible powers behind the thrones of earth, and men are but marionettes, dancing while the invisible ones pull the strings.

We see the dancer, but the master mind that does the work remains concealed by the cloak of silence."

Manly P. Hall
33rd Degree Mason
WHAT THE ANCIENT WISDOM
EXPECTS OF ITS DISCIPLES
page 58

The following individuals named in this book have positively been identified as members of the Masonic Lodge:

John G. Bigelow
Salmon G. Bigelow
John Wilkes Booth
William Andrews Clark
Thomas T. Crittenden
J. Frank Dalton
Att. Gen. Harry M. Daugherty
General Nathan Bedford Forrest
Manly P. Hall
Pres. Warren G. Harding
Jesse Woodson James
Pres. Andrew Johnson
Sen. Robert M. LaFollette
Charles Leadbeater
Albert Pike, "leader of the worldwide
      Masonic movement"
William Clarke Quantrill
Henry H. Rogers
President Franklin Delano Roosevelt
President Theodore (Teddy) Roosevelt
Edwin M. Stanton, Secretary of War in
      Lincoln's cabinet
President Harry Truman
Mark Twain (Samuel L. Clemens)
Arthur Edward Waite

I have put the names of the members of the Masonic Lodge in **BOLD** as a means of assisting the reader in identifying these people throughout the book, and as a way of illustrating that the Masons are the missing ingredient in the Jesse James story. However, since this book is about primarily Jesse James, Frank James and J. Frank Dalton, all members of the Masonic Lodge, I have decided not to BOLD their names just for the sake of making the book more readable.

But know that each of these men were also members of the Masons as you read.

There is circumstantial evidence to support the position that the following individuals were members of either the Masonic Lodge or The Knights of the Golden Circle:

"Bloody Bill" Anderson
Allen Pinkerton

The "circumstantial evidence" consists of photographs of the two men giving what are clearly hand signs with their right hands. (The pictures have been reproduced on page 139.)

These two men are giving the identical signs given by both Jesse and Frank James in that photograph of Jesse and Frank standing side by side with their right hands upon their coat lapels. (This photo has been reproduced on page 137.)

The following individuals are NOT members of the Masonic Lodge, at least as far as I was able to determine:

> Abraham Lincoln
> William H. Seward
> Lt. General Philip Sheridan

I want to certify that I am not a Mason and have never been a member of any Masonic Lodge, nor have I ever applied to be a member.

But I have read their literature, something any serious researcher can do, because it is available to the non-member.

> Ralph Epperson

Every other name in this book has been checked against a four volume set of books entitled 10,000 FAMOUS FREEMASONS, by William R. Denslow, and published in 1957 by Macoy Publishing & Masonic Supply Company, in Richmond, Virginia.

While it does not appear that Macoy Publishing Company is an OFFICIAL source of material on the Masonic Lodge, their catalog states that they have provided "OVER 145 YEARS OF SERVICE TO THE FRATERNAL ORGANIZATIONS," and their official name on their catalog includes their connection to the Masons (see the underlined above.)

NO OTHER NAME MENTIONED in this book is listed among the 10,000 MASONS, as far as I could determine.

The following individuals have uncertain (or unknown) membership in the Masonic Lodge:

Charlie Bigelow   Charlie Ford
*William H. Bonney   Robert (Bob) Ford
   (Billy the Kid)   *Pat Garrett
Jack Burns   Tom Hinds
Marcus Daly   Ed O'Kelly
A. B. Ford

* I have been unable to locate any evidence that Billy the Kid and/or Pat Garrett were members of the Masonic Lodge.

But I also believe that Billy was not shot by Mr. Garrett as history has recorded. One reason could be that they were both Masons and they worked out an arrangement to protect each other, because Masons take oaths to protect their brothers in the Lodge. This would explain why "Brushy Bill" Roberts could claim that he was the real Billy the Kid many years later and the fact that Pat Garrett never claimed the reward money for the shooting of Billy.

INTRODUCTION

This book, first published as a 51 page booklet in 1993, is being updated in the period of June through September of the year 2000, just months after the search for the body of J. Frank Dalton, the man who claimed to be Jesse James, began. Then I added even further comments in the year 2003 to further document my case. And I added more in 2005.

The grave of Mr. Dalton has not been found as of this date (September of 2000, nor as of 2003, nor 2005) so I cannot comment on the test results of that individual's DNA.

However, I am convinced that Mr. Dalton was the legendary outlaw, Jesse James, and because of that conviction, I am releasing this update of the book that I first wrote in 1993.

However, as I wrote in my booklet in 1993, I want you to know that I am convinced that the man in the grave, when it is found, will be the real Jesse James, and that is why I am updating the book that gave you that evidence back then: to bring you additional information that I have found since that year.

> Ralph Epperson
> the author

AUTHOR'S PREFACE

The story you are about to read is true. At least it is as true as far as one can determine from a story that was told over 50 years ago. It is a story about Jesse James, an individual who lived during a time when there were reporters and authors writing about him that were intended to make Jesse into a "bigger than life" hero of "the old west."

It has been estimated that more than 450 dime novels were written about "the James Boys" (meaning brothers Jesse and Frank James) from 1888 to 1900. Many of these writers embellished the truth, or changed the story, or made up details, all in an effort to make their works more entertaining and therefore more marketable. That certainly makes it difficult to sort out the truth from all of their falsehoods.

Therefore, this story is as true as one can determine since all of the principals are no longer living to tell their side of the story and the reporters who wrote the stories have all closed their notepads and they can no longer verify or deny their claims.

If this story is true as I claim, it will have to rank as one of the greatest stories of our time. If the man who told the story about his being Jesse James, America's most famous outlaw, after he was supposedly dead for some 60 years, was telling the truth, the writings about what modern historians call "The Civil War" and "the old west" will have to be rewritten.

Tragically, it appears as if all of the people who were listening to this man tell his story in the late 1940's and early 1950's, did not fully comprehend the enormity of what he was saying. It is a real tragedy that no one who understood THE

CONSPIRATORIAL VIEW OF HISTORY (the view that holds that the major events of the day are planned years in advance by a central conspiracy) met the man telling the story at the time he was telling it. Because if someone had, history as it is recorded today would have been written differently.

Because if this man who claimed to be Jesse James was telling the truth, and my research contends that he was, Jesse James was one of the major players in America's past. If this story is true, Jesse James consorted with some of the most powerful people in America between the period of 1861, the beginning of the Civil War, and 1951, when he passed away.

But what you are about to read is only a glimpse into one part of the entire story. This book has been written about only one of this man's many claims, the claim that the man who said he was Jesse James lived part of his life under the alias of **William Andrews Clark**.

Because **William Andrews Clark** was a (somewhat) visible figure in the history of that period. He had a public life, and people could identify him and write about his story.

In fact, author Herbert V. Young, the secretary to the general manager of Jerome's United Verde Copper Company, (a company owned by Mr. Clark at one time,) from 1912 to 1955, wrote this about Mr. Clark on pages 35 - 36 of his book entitled THEY CAME TO JEROME:

> "The Senator [**William Andrews Clark** was a U.S. Senator from Montana, from 1901 - 1907,] it was claimed, had become the richest man in the world, having surpassed in wealth such plutocrats as the Astors, the Vanderbilts, the Rockefellers, the Goulds, the Rothschilds, and all other men who had loomed large

in the world of money."

This means, if I am right, that Jesse James was a major player in the history of not only the United States, but in the world as well. A man with this sort of wealth takes on power like a man puts on a raincoat during a storm.

The life of Jesse James, however, has been basically kept hidden and concealed. How this man spent his time on earth was kept secret by himself and those around him. It appears as if Jesse did not want the public to know who he was nor what it was that he was doing under this or any one of the other 71 aliases he assumed during his lifetime.

That is, until May 19, 1948, when a man by the name of J. Frank Dalton surfaced in Oklahoma and claimed to be the legendary Jesse James.

I have done a fair amount of research into this story, and all of the material I have found so far has convinced me that Mr. Dalton was telling the truth. However, there is still research to be done and I am hoping that this book will encourage additional research by others into Mr. Dalton's claims. And as a part of that study, I have been in contact with Mr. Bud Hardcastle, a researcher from Oklahoma who has been studying the entire story of the man named Dalton for some 25 years, and he is encouraging me to continue my research into this one part of the full story.

Mr. Hardcastle is the gentleman who started the process of proving or disproving the claims of J. Frank Dalton in Granbury, Texas, in May of 2000 by first obtaining the support of relatives of Jesse James, and then getting court permission to open the grave of Mr. Dalton to exhume his body and remove parts of it for DNA testing.

When I asked Mr. Hardcastle if he believed that the essential ingredients of this particular part of the entire story were true, (meaning the claim that Dalton was not only Jesse James but also the legendary **William Andrews Clark**) he immediately stated that he was, as far as the 25 years of his life, thousands of hours of first hand interviews, and countless hours spent reading the works of those involved in looking into this story, could take him. He stated that he has talked to many of the relatives of the principals in the story, in the recent past, and they have convinced him that Dalton's claims were correct.

But the reader of my book is cautioned to be aware that this is a story told by a man claiming to be Jesse James, and Jesse was known as a man who often had little interest in the truth. This man claimed that he had assumed the identities of 72 various people during his 103 years on this earth, one of which is the major subject of this book. So it certainly could be stated that he did not tell the truth in this story just as he had not told the truth about who he really was.

That is why I have included some of the photographs that I have assembled in the past showing the many faces of the three individuals involved in the story (the old man who claimed to be Jesse James, the historical **William Andrews Clark,** and the young Jesse James) in the approximate center of the book so that the reader can compare them for themselves.

So the reader is encouraged to open up as if they had been empaneled on a jury that was being asked to examine the evidence offered. And as a jury member, you have been admonished to weigh the evidence honestly and fairly before you reach a verdict.

Because how you handle the story told by J. Frank Dalton

after you complete your reading of my book will determine how historians handle the life of Jesse James in the future.

Because I am convinced that J. Frank Dalton was telling the truth when he claimed to be the real Jesse James.

Ralph Epperson
the author

chapter one
JESSE JAMES
FOLK HERO

Few in America have not heard the name of Jesse James, the famous outlaw. He is perhaps this nation's most famous criminal, having been the subject of countless books, novels, movies and documentaries.

Jesse has been made out to be a "folk hero," larger than life, especially during the time he was alive. The people of Missouri, the state he grew up in, had been told during this time that he was "a Robin Hood, robbing the rich to give to the poor." Stories circulated about how he helped the widows of fallen Southern soldiers in the Civil War and how he robbed the banks and trains belonging to Northerners who the citizens of the South felt had been stealing from them after the war had ended.

Perhaps the greatest example of this is this story, often repeated by those who believed that Jesse was a "good man turned wrong by the times." This story has many versions, but I believe this one was perhaps the most commonly told.

The story has Jesse and his older brother Frank returning from the Civil War. They needed to water their horses and stopped at the farm belonging to a Confederate soldier's widow.

She was crying because the sheriff was coming later that day to collect $300 in back mortgage payments that the widow did not have.

Jesse, feeling compassion for the widow's needs, gave her $300 to give to the sheriff when he appeared. They recommended that she obtain a receipt from the sheriff for the money after she had paid it. He and Frank then rode a little distance from the farm and hid in some bushes.

The James brothers watched as the sheriff rode up and visited the farm. They watched as he collected the $300 from the widow, issued her a receipt, and then started to return to the city. Jesse and Frank stepped into his path and robbed him of the $300 and then allowed the sheriff to leave unharmed.

This was somewhat typical of the type of portrayal of the James brothers that the people of the time received from a generally friendly press.

Another example of such thoughts about the character of Jesse was a little more recent, but it still shows that this story was handed down to more modern observers. This is a recording of what President **Harry S. Truman** said about Jesse James, his fellow Missourian, on March 27, 1949:

> "Jesse James was not actually a bad man at heart. I have studied his life carefully, and I come from his part of the country. Jesse James was a modern-day Robin Hood. He stole from the rich and gave to the poor, which, in general, is not a bad policy." THE COMPLETE AND AUTHENTIC LIFE OF JESSE JAMES, PAGE 45

It probably would not have made any difference to the President, but **Truman**'s comment that Robin Hood was one who "stole from the rich to give to the poor" is not a fair summary of the story of this legendary outlaw. It might be remembered that Robin was taking back the taxes that had been collected from the poor by the government of the King and the Sheriff of Nottingham. He was not stealing from the rich, unless you would contend that the rich were in control of the government at the time and were somehow receiving some of the stolen tax monies.

But, at the very least, Robin was not stealing from the rich to give to the poor. He was taking back that which had been taken from the poor by the government through taxation. And basically, neither was Jesse James.

History has recorded another incident on January 26, 1875 that also built enormous sympathy for Jesse and his brother Frank James.

It was on that night that history has recorded the bombing of the James farmhouse by the Pinkerton National Detective Agency in an attempt to flush out the James brothers from inside the home. (There is some disagreement amongst historians about whether either or both of the James brothers were in the home that night. I would say that most believe that they were not there that night.)

But, in any event, the bomb that the Pinkertons threw into the home exploded and blew off the lower right arm of Zarelda James, Jesse's mother, and killed Jesse's half-brother, 7 year old Archie Samuel, the son of Zarelda and her third husband, Dr. Reuben Samuel.

It is now known that Pinkerton intended to burn the house down during that raid. He wrote a letter dated December 28, 1874 that has been copied in its entirety by Ted Yeatman in his book. Part of that letter reads as follows:

"Above every thing destroy the house, blot it from the

face of the earth. Here the logs will burn [the James farm house was constructed in part of logs] the house down." (Page 131 of Yeatman's book)

Visitors to the James farm today can see the evidence that the house was set on fire. Part of the outside wall still shows this fire damage.

This was also confirmed in another letter written by Allan Pinkerton, this one dated January 27, 1875:

". . . at about half past twelve midnight we commenced firing the buildings."

So the intent was not only to capture the James brothers, it was also to destroy the house that the James family lived in. Obviously, both attempts failed: they did not burn the house down nor did they capture or kill the James brothers.

But as a result of this act, public sentiment turned against the Pinkertons and in favor of Jesse and his brother Frank.

It was not until 1992 that official U.S. government records were examined and they revealed that the bomb the privately owned Pinkerton Agency (it wasn't federal!) used in the James home had been secured at a U.S. Arsenal at Rock Island, Illinois. That means that the bomb that was thrown into the James home was obtained from the U.S. government.

This use of government military materials against the citizens of the United States became the subject of a law passed June 18, 1878 and known as the Posse Comitatus Act. This law makes it illegal for the U.S. government to use military forces or equipment against the people of the United States. The Army cannot have anything to do with civil law enforcement.

Of course, this law was passed after the bombing of the James home, but it showed that legislators later decided such an act as committed by the U.S. Arsenal would have been illegal if the Pinkerton's bombing had been perpetrated a few years later.

Marley Brant further discusses this "bomb" in his book entitled JESSE JAMES THE MAN AND THE MYTH on page 136:

> "Dated December 30, 1874, an entry in the Rock Island Arsenal registry of letters posts a note from Lieutenant General Philip Sheridan in which he introduces Robert J. Linden:

> '. . . one of Pinkerton's Detective Police, who wishes to obtain certain materials from Rock Island Arsenal, to aid him in arresting certain railroad robbers.'"

Carl Breihan provided his readers with additional details about the object thrown into the James home. This is how he described it: (page 75)

> "a thirty-three pound iron bomb filled with gunpowder was thrown into the room, wrapped in flaming, kerosene saturated rags."

Ralph Dudley, the general manager of the Pinkerton Agency at the time, gave Homer Croy an interview that he published in his book JESSE JAMES WAS MY NEIGHBOR. This is the official Pinkerton response:

> "Our men had with them a device for illuminating a darkened place. It was something akin in nature to the firepots which later came to be used on highways. The

31

contents were probably kerosene and turpentine."

But the article in 1992 that appeared in The Arizona Daily Star, my local newspaper, stated that "a Pinkerton agent got a BOMB [Epperson's emphasis] from the U.S. Arsenal in Rock Island, Illinois."

All we know for certain is that whatever it was, it exploded and severely damaged the right arm of Zarelda and killed her son Archie.

The public will have to decide for themselves.

But, even today, interest in the outlaw Jesse James remains high, even as it does with the other legendary outlaw, Robin Hood.

In fact, just a few years ago, on April 29, 1993, the .44 caliber Smith and Wesson revolver that supposedly was used to kill Jesse in 1882 was sold at a public auction for $164,000. (There is some dispute that this was the gun that Ford "shot Jesse" with. A gentleman who was in St, Joseph, Missouri, close enough to have heard the shot, said he was told it was a .45 Colt revolver that Ford allegedly used.) So interest in the man continues even though his supposed death occurred over a hundred years ago.

And almost everyone who has heard about Jesse has heard the now famous story of how he was murdered in 1882. In fact, there was even a popular song written about him that made that story a part of America's past.

But if the story you are about ready to read is true, all of the historians who have repeated that story of his "death," have not been completely honest with the public, nor have they been thorough in their research. Because the story that follows is the story about how Jesse James did not die in 1882 when he was 35 but lived to be 103 years of age.

There is no way for me to determine whether some of these writers knew that what they were telling the American people was not the truth, but it would be fair to say that there certainly were stories circulating at the time that Jesse had not died in the famous shooting that supposedly took his life, and that honest efforts could have been made to develop and then expose the truth.

But conversely, there was much to be gained by not having the truth told. Jesse, his family and his fellow gang members, wanted the story that the outlaw had been killed to continue being told just as it was being circulated, for reasons that will be discussed later.

And those who heard the rumors certainly could have claimed that if they had started the process to discover the truth that Jesse was alive, they could have been murdered themselves for digging into a story that was supposed to be as dead as Jesse was supposed to be. So fear at the time might have prevented the truth from being told.

And this writer can certainly understand that, because Jesse was known to be a murderer. And he had a very loyal gang around him. And if reporters were digging into the story to declare that he had not died as his family, gang members, the news media and government officials had declared, they might not have survived themselves.

So it is easy to write that the story of his shooting is not true from the safety of a vantage point of over 100 years past the actual event. And this writer is aware of that.

But this story is so enormous that even this current writer is fearful of making it public. There are people alive today who understandably do not want the story to be told, and others who are descendants of some of the members of the same conspiracies that Jesse belonged to that will be discussed later in this book who do not want the story to be made public either.

But this writer has decided to expose the truth to the American people, as far as I have found it.

It is time that the American people are told a little of the concealed truth about their past.

It is time to tell the truth about two of America's most legendary men: Jesse James and Senator **William Andrews Clark**.

chapter two
JESSE JAMES, MOVIE STAR

The story of Jesse James is many things, but it is not about the real Jesse being a movie star!

But a part of the story is about the many movies that have been made ABOUT Jesse!

Because I have an interest in this story, I have watched as many of these movies as I can find. And there is almost always one constant in all of the ones that I have watched: THE WRITERS SIMPLY CHANGE THE STORY LINE! And there does not seem to be a reason for doing so! Someone just changes the information known to be true, for some reason unknown to the viewer.

I would like to comment on five of these films, by specifically listing the errors the screen writers allowed to be included in the story line. This will not be an exhaustive list of the errors, only a brief one that I made as I watched each movie. I certainly could have missed some mistakes, so I only will list those that I found to be the most glaring as I watched.

I will not provide the name of the movie, as this is not an attempt to be critical of the particular movie, it is an attempt to be critical of Hollywood in general!

And the reason is important: movies about Jesse James simply cannot be relied upon for true information about the James story.

The first movie of the five was made in 1939, and contained the most errors of all of the five I viewed.

This one made the following mistakes: (I will list the mistake and then explain what the truth is, at least what the historians writing about the Jesse James story have found as being the truth:)

1. The James farm in the movie is a two story house (the James farm still exists and is currently a museum. It is a one story building.)
2. The name of the town nearest to the farm in the movie is called Liberty (the town is named Kearney. Liberty appears to be about 5 to 8 miles southeast of Kearney.
3. It is railroad men who come onto the James farm to force the family to sell their property at a reduced price. Jesse and Frank are both at home.(As far as my research has gone, the only intrusion on the James farm was NOT from railroad men, but from Northern soldiers looking for Frank James, who was fighting with **Quantrill**'s Raiders at the time.)
4. This scene with the railroad men was supposed to have been AFTER the Civil War was over, (but by that time Jesse and Frank were generally living away from the house.)
5. Zarelda James, the mother of Frank and Jesse, dies shortly after the confrontation with the railroad men. (Zarelda died in 1911, about 40 years after the event.)
6. The railroad man in charge throws the "smoke bomb" into the James farmhouse. (It was the Pinkerton Detective men who threw not a SMOKE BOMB, but a REAL BOMB into the house.)
7. The home where Jesse James was shot in 1882 is also a two story home. (The real house still exists today, as a museum in St. Joseph, Missouri and is a one story

house.)

8. It was Bob Ford, the man who later shot Jesse James, who informed some authorities about the Northfield, Minnesota bank robbery. (There is no evidence that Bob Ford did such a thing.)

9. It appears in the movie that Jesse and Frank James were the only ones to escape the robbery. (All three of the Youngers in the gang and both of the James brothers that held up the bank survived the shooting after the robbery that killed at least two of the other robbers.)

10. Zee James, the wife of Jesse James, has only one child at the time of the shooting of Jesse. (She had two children.)

11. Bob and Charlie Ford leave the house and then open the outside door and fired TWO shots at Jesse, killing him. (It was Bob Ford who fired only ONE shot at Jesse, from inside the living room of the house.)

The second movie was made in 1980:

1 The Pinkerton detectives who throw the bomb into the James house claim that it was NOT a bomb, but some sort of smoke bomb, intended on driving Jesse and Frank out of the house. (It was clearly a bomb, and was intended to burn the house down.)

2. The bomb kills Jesse's 15 year old half-brother, Archie Samuel, a "simpleton." (Archie was 9.)

3. When Bob Ford shoots Jesse James, he does not stand on a chair. (The official story is that Jesse stood on a chair.)

4. Jesse was apparently aware of the plot to shoot him, because just before it happens, he says "goodby" to his son in the kitchen. (There is not one shred of evidence to support this conclusion.)

5.   It appears as if Jesse allowed himself to be murdered. (There is NOT one shred of evidence in the official story that Jesse was aware he was going to be shot.)

6.   Frank James surrenders to the sheriff after the death of Jesse James. (Frank does surrender to the authorities many years later, but it is not the sheriff he surrenders to, it is to Thomas Crittenden, the Governor of Missouri.)

7.   There is one cryptic scene as the movie ends, that would tend to force the viewer to another conclusion: as Frank James takes the body of Jesse to be buried (there is NO record of this happening in the official story) the train he is riding in passes a solitary figure standing on the side of the railroad tracks. Is this the way the producers are telling you that the figure was the still alive Jesse?

The third movie was made in 1994:

1.   The railroad men come to Jesse's farm in 1869, four years after the Civil War. (There is no information that this event ever took place.)

2   The James farm house is once again a two story. (The real house is one story.)

3.   As I remember, the railroad men shoot Jesse's step father, Dr. Samuel. (There is no record of this event ever happening.)

4.   Charlie Ford, as a gang member, is shot by Alan Pinkerton, the owner of the detective agency hunting the James brothers. (There is no record of this event ever happening either.)

The fourth movie was made more in 2001:

1.   The Pinkerton men actually burn the entire house

down. (The James farm house is still standing, and is currently a museum.)

2.   This event killed Zarelda James, the mother of Jesse and Frank James. (Zarelda lived to 1911.)
3.   The Pinkerton's arrested Jesse James and took him to Washington D.C. (There is no record of this ever taking place.)

The date of the fifth movie was not shown on the advertising material accompanying the movie:

1.   The bomb thrown by the Pinkerton men was a "smoke bomb" intending to force the inhabitants out. (The bomb was a real bomb, intended to burn the house down.)
2.   Jesse suspects he is going to be shot in the living room and he steps up on a chair to allow this to happen. (There is NOT ONE SHRED of evidence that this happened.)
3.   The picture that Jesse was "straightening" as he stood on the chair was a picture of a race horse. (The real framed picture was a cloth with words inscribed on it.)

So the lesson is clear:

if you want the truth about the Jesse James story, you might not choose to GO TO THE MOVIES for it!

chapter three
THE BEGINNING

The headline of the Lawton, Oklahoma *CONSTITUTION* newspaper for the date of May 19, 1948 read:

JESSE JAMES IS ALIVE!
IN LAWTON

It is quite probable that the majority of the people who read that headline were skeptical of the truth of that statement, because the commonly accepted story from the past held that Jesse James had been murdered in 1882, about 66 years before.

But the articles that accompanied the headline claimed that he was alive, in Lawton, and "riding the trails again." They stated that the man making the claims called himself Colonel J. Frank Dalton, and that he had suddenly appeared in the city claiming to be the famous outlaw Jesse James, the "Robin Hood of the post Civil War era."

And the reason Mr. Dalton was making that claim was because he and some of the other leaders of the Knights of the Golden Circle, a Civil War group Jesse belonged to, had promised each other that the first one to reach 100 years of age would tell the truth. And Mr. Dalton had reached 100 in 1947.

Dalton claimed that he was born on September 5, 1847, as the second son of Rev. Robert Sallee James, a Baptist minister, and Zarelda Cole James. Their first son was Alexander Franklin James, commonly called Frank James, born on January 10, 1843.

It is important at this time to make certain that the reader understands just who this man Dalton claimed to be.

He signed "AN AFFIDAVIT" on April 24th, 1948 that read, in part:

> "I, J. Frank Dalton, wish to state that I am the son of Robert James, a Baptist minister, and Zarelda Cole, and that I was born at Centerville [the original name of KEARNEY,] Missouri, on September 5th, 1847.
>
> My real name is and always has been JESSE WOODSON JAMES. My full brother was ALEXANDER FRANK JAMES, four years older than myself." (Unnumbered page, approx. p. 6, in the beginning of JESSE JAMES RIDES AGAIN)

Homer Croy in his book entitled JESSE JAMES WAS MY NEIGHBOR stated that "the James family Bible" supported this claim. The Bible was owned by the parents (Zarelda and Robert,) and then passed on to Frank James, their first son, and then to his son named Robert James. This Bible is currently on display at the James Farm and Museum in Kearney, the former home of the James family.

That Bible contains a list of, as Croy called them, "THE PRINCIPALS IN THE DRAMA," the 16 names of the family members who were directly involved with the James family. It reads as follows (I have reduced this list to the essentials, meaning those who are directly involved in the James, Clark and Dalton story:)

41

NAME	BORN / DIED
Robert S. James (Jesse's father)	July 17, 1818 Aug. 18, 1850
Zarelda Cole James (Jesse's mother)	Jan. 29, 1825 Feb. 10, 1911
Alexander Frank James (Jesse's brother)	Jan. 10, 1843 Feb. 18, 1915
Jesse Woodson James (the real Jesse)	Sept. 5, 1847 April 3, 1882
Susie James (Jesse's sister)	Nov. 25, 1849 March 3, 1889
Archie Payton Samuels (Jesse's half brother)	July 26, 1866 Jan. 26, 1875
Zarelda Mimms James	(?), 1845 Nov. 30, 1900

(Jesse's wife; apparently the date of her birth was unknown to the James family)

(This Bible listing becomes important in resolving the question of whether or not Jesse WOODSON James was the real son of Zarelda and Robert. There are some researchers into the James story who are claiming that the real son of this couple was Jesse ROBERT James. They base their conclusion, in part, on the 1850 United States Census.

This author has seen a copy of that census and it lists the names of the James family something like this:

> JAMES, Robert Sallee
> JAMES, Zarelda
> JAMES, Alexander Frank
> JAMES, Jesse R. (Notice the census form says his middle initial was "R" and not "W")

One possible explanation for this contradiction is that, unlike

42

today when the Census Bureau mails out the census forms to the individual homeowner, who completes it, and then returns it to the Bureau, it appears that the 1850 census was conducted by a census taker who visited each of the households in the neighborhood and obtained the information that was then brought back to another census worker who listed the results by family on a sheet of paper. It was this second person's responsibility to correctly prepare the master list showing each family, in alphabetical order by the family head.

A careful examination of the whole page listing the James family shows that the page appears to have been written by one person. And James, Robert, and his family, is shown just before James, Ronald, and his family (for example.)

So it is possible that the compiler could have made a mistake by not reading the census taker's writing correctly and simply put down an "R" instead of the correct "W" as a middle initial. At best, that is a possible explanation for the "R" on the sheet. No one knows for certain except the page compiler, and to my knowledge no one ever put that person's explanation for the discrepancy on the list into writing.)

But let me return to the family record in the Bible.

It would be almost inconceivable for the public to be asked to believe that Robert James, Jesse's father and an ordained Christian Minister, well known in his area and one who helped found William Jewell College in Liberty, Missouri, would have listed a son in a Holy Bible as Jesse Woodson James when his son was really named Jesse Robert James.

Before the day of the American Birth Certificate, (I have read where it was in 1901 that families had to obtain a birth certificate for their newly born children) families used the Bible as the "official record" of family births, deaths and marriages. So, this became the official record for the family, and why Rev. Robert would make such a mistake, if he did, in his family's "official record," is beyond comprehension.

So let this be the official declaration based upon the family Bible: Jesse Woodson James was the second son of Zarelda and Robert James.

Secondly, this listing of Zarelda Mimms' name (although her name was Zarelda, her family and friends called her Zee) in the Bible poses another question in the debate as to whom a woman by this name married.

The addition of her name in the listing in the Bible should assist those who believe that it was Jesse James who married a woman by that name because there are others who do not believe Zee married the real Jesse Woodson James.

It certainly would be strange to see the James chronicler write her name in the family Bible if she was not a James family member, even though it was by marriage.

The James family reports that Zarelda (Zee) Mimms, (sometimes spelled Mimmbs) married Jesse Woodson James on April 4, 1874. And that is why her name is included in the family Bible.

But there is another explanation as to why her name is in the James family Bible. That explanation will be discussed later in this book.

In the matter of the real name of the second son of the James parents, the 1850 Census List does not clarify the situation, it only adds to the confusion.

But in spite of the disagreements amongst historians, it is fair to conclude that the son of Zarelda and Robert James was Jesse Woodson James.

And the man claiming to be that man was J. Frank Dalton.

It is not known for certain why J. Frank Dalton was using the last name of Dalton when he appeared in Oklahoma, but one possible explanation comes with the theory that his mother Zarelda and her sister had been born as Daltons, but that their father had died when they were around 2 and 4 years of age. They were reportedly placed into a Catholic convent until they were adopted by a family named Cole.

This theory was given partial support by a report by Carl W. Breihan in his book entitled THE COMPLETE AND AUTHENTIC LIFE OF JESSE JAMES. This is what he reported about Rev. Robert:

> "The Preacher [had] received his training in the Georgetown, Kentucky, College . . . [and] he fell in love with Zarelda Cole, a girl in a Catholic convent in Lexington [Kentucky.]" (page 68)

Rudy Turilli, the man who spent an enormous amount of time with J. Frank Dalton after he surfaced in 1948, wrote a booklet entitled THE TRUTH ABOUT JESSE JAMES. In it, he discussed the claim made by Ola Everhard, the niece of Jesse James, that Zarelda James was born a Dalton:

> "Zarelda, mother of Frank and Jesse James, is referred to in most annals as Zarelda E. Cole, prior to her marriage to Robert James.
>
> She was born Zarelda E. Dalton -- and Mrs. Everhard

has the answer, from information handed down in the family.

The father of the Dalton girls [Zarelda had a sister named Sarah] died when they were very young [he died on February 27, 1827] [the book entitled JESSE AND FRANK JAMES adds another detail in his death by reporting that Zarelda was two when her father was 'killed in a horse accident.'] (page 35)

They were Roman Catholic, and Mrs. Dalton, the mother, placed them in a convent. After she married a man named Cole, the girls returned home and it meant not only a new life for them but a new name as well.

They took the name of their stepfather Cole."

William A. Settle Jr., in his book entitled JESSE JAMES WAS HIS NAME, added yet another bit of information about this time in Zarelda's life:

". . . Zarelda was attending school at a Roman Catholic convent in Lexington where her guardian James M. Lindsay had placed her." (Page 6)

The fact that Zarelda had a guardian implies that her mother had given her and presumably her sister up to someone else after her husband had died. And it was he who had given the two sisters to the nuns in the convent to raise until he could arrange for their adoption. And apparently the convent did that by allowing the Cole family to adopt the two sisters.

Still another who wrote about these days in the convent was Carl W. Breihan in his book entitled THE DAY JESSE

JAMES WAS KILLED:

"While a student there [Georgetown College, in Kentucky] he [Robert Salle James] fell in love with an orphan girl named Zarelda Cole, a Scott County child who had been raised in a Catholic convent in Lexington." (Page 21)

This story was amplified by Joe Wood in his book on Jesse James. This is how he discussed it after he met with Ola Everhard in Austin, Texas while J. Frank was still alive:

"Mrs. Everhard's great-grandmother was Sarah (Sallie) Dalton [this is the sister of Zarelda] before her marriage to Henry Underwood.

One of the sisters of Sarah Dalton was Zarelda Dalton, who married Robert James and was the mother of Jesse W. James, according to the family Bible.

The father of the Dalton girls died when they were very young. [And then Mr. Wood repeats the comments made by Mrs. Everhard.] They were Roman Catholic, and Mrs. Dalton placed them in a convent.

After she married a man named Cole, the girls returned home and it meant not only a new life for them but a new name as well.

They took the name of their stepfather Cole."

This information seems to imply that the story of her being born a Dalton and then placed in a Catholic convent is true.

And if J. Frank Dalton believed that, and was in truth the real

47

Jesse Woodson James, it would certainly explain why he chose the last name of Dalton in his later years. It would also explain why he chose the name "J. Frank" as well: the "J" stood for Jesse, and the Frank would refer to his brother Frank James.

Therefore, in one name, he would have included his entire family: his mother through her true last name, his brother through his real name, and the first initial of the name of his true identity.

J. Frank Dalton's name appears to conceal his true identity.

chapter four
THE DEATH OF
THE FATHER

The James family Bible shows that Robert, the husband of
Zarelda and the father to Frank, Jesse and his sister Susan,
died after 1850.

There are some differing explanations of how and why he
died.

The official story is that he left the family on April 12, 1851
to go gold prospecting in California after "the Gold Rush of
1848."

One of the writers on Jesse James suggested he left because
"Zarelda did not share Robert's enthusiasm for the ministry."
(JESSE JAMES WAS HIS NAME, Settle, page 7) This is a
clue that there was some discord in the marriage and that
Robert possibly was leaving because his marriage was in
trouble.

This is how Marley Brant discussed it in his book JESSE
JAMES THE MAN AND THE MYTH: pages 9 and 10:

> "In early spring 1850, Robert James surprised Zarelda
> by informing her that he wanted to follow his brother
> Drury [Drury Woodson James] west to the California
> gold fields.
>
> Other tales have suggested that Zarelda was not faith-
> ful to Robert and that he discovered that Jesse was not

his son after all but rather the result of Zarelda's tryst with a local doctor.

He joined his close friend William Stigers on the journey west to California on April 12, 1851."

This idea that Jesse and Frank were not brothers, but only half-brothers was repeated in the book entitled JESSE JAMES - - THE OUTLAW by Henry J. Walker. (Page 22) This is what he wrote:

"Some years ago this writer learned from an authentic source that Jesse and Frank James were only half-brothers. Also, excerpts from the book THE BORDER OUTLAW by J.W. Buell, bear out this fact. I quote from Buell, whose book was published in 1880:

'It is asserted by those who knew them best, that Jesse and Frank are only half-brothers, having the same mother. The father of Jesse was a physician in Clay County, Missouri.'"

Phillip Steele in his book entitled JESSE AND FRANK JAMES told how Robert, Jesse's father and Zarelda's husband, died: (page 39)

"Robert became ill from food poisoning or some type of fever in a Placerville [California] gold camp and died suddenly on August 18, 1851 [at the age of thirty-two.] He was buried in an unmarked grave."

One of the reasons that Mr. Steel said that he was buried in an "unmarked grave" is because Jesse and Frank went to Placerville years later to locate his grave but were unable to find it:

"Frank joined Jesse in Northern California upon Jesse's arrival there since later accounts by the brothers indicate that they looked for their father's grave together sometime in 1868. Jesse and Frank were still not able to locate the grave of Reverend James." JESSE JAMES: THE MAN AND THE MYTH, page 73

One possible explanation could be this:

Robert James was a Christian minister, the pastor of his church, and highly respected in his community. Let us presume that he discovered that Zarelda had conceived Jesse outside of their marriage vows. It is quite conceivable that he would have felt disgraced in the eyes of the church he pastored and in the city of Kearney, so he concocted the story that he had gone to Placerville and then mysteriously died but a few months later. This would explain the fact that his two sons could not find his grave in Placerville.

It is conceivable that this trip would have eliminated his guilt about having married a woman who had had an affair outside of their marriage. And it would also explain why his two sons could not find his grave years later: he had not died in Placerville in 1851, but faked his death so that he could continue living, perhaps under an assumed name. (Is this how his son Jesse learned the same tactic he used at least twice in his life?)

History has not provided the researcher with the answers, so only speculation can be the result.

But this explanation seems to fit the evidence.

Jesse and Frank were not full brothers: they had the same mother but different fathers.

chapter five
THE SHOOTING IN
ST. JOSEPH

Part of the song about the shooting of Jesse James in 1882 contains these words:

> *Jesse James had a wife;*
> *She's a mourner all her life;*
> *His children, they were brave.*
> *Oh, the dirty little coward that shot Mr. Howard!*
> *And they laid Jesse James in his grave.*

History has recorded that Jesse was murdered on April 3, 1882 while he was living with his wife and two children in St. Joseph, Missouri under the alias of Thomas Howard. The newspapers the next morning reported that the James family had moved to St. Joseph on November 8, 1881, just about five months before the shooting.

The man who claimed to have shot Jesse was 21 year old Bob Ford, a member of Jesse's gang, who, according to the story, shot Jesse in the back of the head, reportedly behind the right ear, while he was either "dusting off a picture on the wall," or "straightening out a picture on the wall" (some of the details in the story change according to who tells it.)

In an interesting sidelight of the story, it has been reported that Mr. Ford shot Jesse James with a weapon that James had given to him "just a few days before his death." (LIFE AND TIMES OF JESSE AND FRANK JAMES, page 316)

The reader will learn in a later chapter of this book that there is a very interesting reason why Jesse would give Bob Ford a weapon that would be used later to shoot him. (JESSE JAMES RIDES AGAIN, page 8)

Mr. Ford claimed that he was visiting the house that day with his brother Charlie, and that they had come to shoot the famous outlaw and collect the reward of $10,000 offered by **Thomas T. Crittenden**, the governor of Missouri, for the death of Jesse James.

The official story that has been recorded by the historians had it that Jesse James had taken his gun belt off containing the two holsters holding his two guns and laid them on a table (or onto a bed) in the main room of the modest house that he was living in.

Just for the record, Zee James gave this testimony in the coroner's inquest:

"Q: When your husband was killed, was he armed?

A: No, sir. The pistols were lying on the bed under his coat." (The Daily Gazette, April 5, 1882, front page)

So, the American people were led to believe that this famous outlaw had taken his gun-belt off and laid it and the two guns in their holsters down so that he could straighten out or dust a picture hanging on a wall in his living room.

Marley Brant, in his book entitled JESSE JAMES, THE MAN AND THE MYTH, discussed this question about Jesse removing his guns:

"Jesse stretched and removed his guns after he entered the living room. Jesse was always on the alert and remained armed even while in his own house. Taking his guns off was completely out of character for him.

What is hard to explain is why Jesse, paranoid and suspicious, would take off his guns and turn his back on untried and surely less-than-trustworthy acquaintances [meaning the two Ford brothers.]"

History has recorded that Bob Ford was already a gang member in Jesse' gang on the day of the shooting, and that Jesse did not know his brother Charlie. That fact would concern most prudent men, especially those who knew that there was a reward out on them. But Jesse didn't think this was so unusual, at least according to the story. This is why these writers are pondering why Jesse would do such a thing.

Mr. Brant, like other writers, does not explain this mystery; he just asks the question.

Another writer raised the same question. This is from the book entitled THE MANY FACES OF JESSE JAMES: (page 66)

"Numerous theories as to why Jesse would have removed his guns, turned his back to the Fords, stood on a chair, and chosen to dust and straighten a picture have been debated for more than one hundred years and will continue to be a topic of discussion."

This writer did not attempt to explain why Jesse did this either.

The fact that the story has Jesse taking his guns and holster off prior to the shooting was of interest at the Coroner's Inuest. Zee James was asked:

Q: Was he [meaning Jesse James] armed when asleep?

A: Yes, sir, he had pistols under his head always."

This testimony illustrates just how justifiably paranoid Jesse James would have been, with a reward hanging over his head. Here the reader learned that he kept guns with him when he was asleep, yet the official story of his shooting has him taking his guns off in the presence of an outlaw and his brother who was unknown to Jesse.

There is certainly reason for skepticism when we are asked to believe that he took his guns off during the day while we now know that he slept with them under his head during the night. But the revealing thing to notice is that these writers did not attempt to answer the question at the time. Why did they not wonder enough about why he would have done such a thing, and research the answer until they had found an explanation.

But the reader will soon learn that I have an answer for this rather strange behavior on the part of Jesse James. It will follow in a few paragraphs.

After the shooting of Jesse, Bob and Charlie Ford confessed that they had shot the outlaw, and on April 17, two weeks after the shooting, they were arraigned in the Criminal Court of St. Joseph, Missouri. They both pleaded guilty to the charge of First Degree Murder and were sentenced to be hanged on May 19, 1882.

However, the very next day, Missouri Governor **Crittenden** gave both of the brothers a "full and unconditional pardon" for ridding the state of the famous outlaw, and the two Ford brothers were released to freedom..

Bob Ford was later killed in 1892, in Crede, Colorado, by a miner named Ed O'Kelly, in a saloon that Ford owned. Apparently Mr. O'Kelly wanted to be crowned as "the man who shot Bob Ford, the man who shot Jesse James." Others have reported that he shot Ford to gain the attention of a woman that both he and Ford were pursuing.

Now would be an appropriate time to wonder why Frank James, Jesse's brother, did not seek revenge on Bob Ford for killing his brother. He never attempted to shoot Bob Ford and historians have wondered about this for years.

One rather interesting comment about Bob Ford is offered on page 24 of Rudy Turilli's booklet :

"In 1890, [eight years after the shooting of Jesse] Frank James was seen with Bob Ford in Crede, Colorado where Bob had opened a saloon and dance hall with Frank James' help.

IS IT POSSIBLE THAT THE BROTHER OF JESSE JAMES WOULD HAVE ASSOCIATED WITH BOB FORD, the supposed 'dirty little coward who killed Mr. Howard [the alias Jesse James was allegedly using at the time of his death] and then put Jesse in his grave' as history tells us.

I hardly think so."

And the reason seems to be apparent: Frank James knew that

Bob Ford DID NOT shoot his brother! Therefore, he would not need to take revenge against the murderer of Jesse.

There is a report that seems to confirm that Frank James knew that his brother was not shot in the home in St. Joseph, Missouri. This report comes from the St. Joseph newspaper published three days after the shooting:

> "It was reported on the streets late last night that Frank James was in the city determined on vengeance and had viewed the corpse at the undertakers.
>
> It is extremely probable that such is the case and that he received almost immediate notification of the death of his brother, and risking capture had come to take a last look at his brother."

Another writer commented on the presence of Frank James in St. Joseph. That was William A. Settle Jr., who wrote this on page 130 of his book JESSE JAMES WAS HIS NAME:

> "Rumors about Frank were numerous at the time of Jesse's death. These included reports of his presence in St. Joseph immediately after the murder, [and] of his attendance at the funeral . . . .
>
> The belief that he would avenge Jesse's death was widespread."

Since Frank did not take "vengeance" for the death of his "brother," a case could be made that he knew that Jesse had not died in that house. Even if the critic suggests that it is also conceivable that he never had the opportunity because of the large number of people at all of the events surrounding this shooting in St. Joseph, one could quickly point out that Bob

Ford was not shot by anyone until 8 years after the shooting. That would have given Frank ample time to locate Mr. Ford and seek his "vengeance" if he had believed that he had taken the life of his brother.

J. Frank Dalton, the man who in 1948 claimed to be Jesse James, added that the real Bob Ford did not die in this shooting in Colorado, but that it was A.B. Ford, a 6 foot tall "double" who was shot. Dalton claimed that the real Bob Ford later went to work for him in the mining business as his accountant and bookkeeper. He further stated that Ford's son was later elected Governor of Montana, but unfortunately for the sake of history, he did not name this individual.

Bob's brother Charlie also had a violent death. He committed suicide in Richmond, Missouri on May 6, 1884, quite possibly because he couldn't live with the lie any longer.

But the story told by J. Frank Dalton in 1948 about the shooting of Jesse James was quite a bit different.

He claimed that the man killed that day as Jesse James was in fact Charlie Bigelow, a James gang member who had been banished from the gang after it was discovered that he could not be trusted any longer. His story included his claim that it was he, Jesse James, who shot Charlie Bigelow.

(In a previous portion of this book, I commented on the fact that Bob Ford, the man who "shot Jesse James," mentioned that the gun he used to do the shooting had been given to him by Jesse himself just a "few days before his death."

If Dalton's version of the shooting is correct, then he would have had to give the gun he used to shoot Bigelow with to Ford because Ford would need it to confirm that it was the weapon that he used to shoot the outlaw. If the bullet that killed James had been found and if it came from a gun of a different caliber than the one Bob Ford had in his possession, the sheriff would have known that he could not have been the one who shot Jesse James.

So, Dalton (James) had to give Ford the gun he used to shoot Bigelow to make certain that there was no question that Ford had done the shooting, because the gun that had been used to shoot Jesse had to be in Ford's possession.

But back to the issue of Bigelow not being a trusted gang member.)

One who made this observation that Bigelow was a gang member was Joe Wood, a photojournalist for the St. Louis Globe-Democrat newspaper for 30 years until he retired. He met J. Frank Dalton while he was alive during the years of 1948 to 1951. He wrote a 32 page booklet entitled MY JESSE JAMES STORY in which he wrote his observations of the story surrounding Mr. Dalton. He made this comment about Charlie Bigelow:

> "A man who Jesse suspected of spying for the Pinkerton detective agency . . . ."

He amplified his thoughts a little later in the same book:

> "The Pinkerton Detective Agency, working for the railroads had offered a $10,000 reward for the capture of Jesse James, dead or alive. This prompted the plot to kill Bigelow, have his body identified and buried as Jesse James."

One who supplied some additional insight as to why Jesse

could not trust Charlie was James R. Davis, a long time friend of Dalton's. This is what he said in a recorded interview as published on page 45 of Rudy Turilli's book:

"That was Tom Bigelow who was killed and he got in there by one of Pinkerton's men, -- I said Tom Bigelow, that's Charlie Bigelow -- on account that he was an outlaw and he got in there to turn up [apparently "turn up" means to betray someone else or to turn that party into the legal authorities] the James Boys and the gang, and the reason he was killed, . . . when he was in there as a spy to turn 'em up.'"

This thought was continued in Joe Wood's book as he extended the remarks made by Mr. Davis:

"Charlie Bigelow had been planted in the Jesse James gang to turn up the whole business the first opportunity he had as to where they were at."

"Bigelow, who was known to be working for the Pinkertons disappeared and was never heard from again." [Of course, this is what you would expect if Dalton shot Charlie that day. I will discuss what I think Mr. Davis meant by this comment in a later chapter of this book when I discuss the Northfield, Minnesota bank robbery.]

These thoughts were echoed in another book, JESSE JAMES RIDES AGAIN by Frank O. Hall and Lindsey H. Whitten, the two newspaper reporters who did the original research in Lawton, Oklahoma after Frank Dalton appeared in their city. This is how they discussed Charlie Bigelow:

"The man who was killed was . . . Charlie Bigelow, a

former member of the gang who later started giving certain information of Jesse's activities to officers of the law." P. 7 JESSE JAMES RIDES AGAIN.

Apparently Charlie Bigelow was using the name of Jesse James as he robbed trains and stages. In fact, it appears as if Charlie had a gang of his own doing exactly that, if the following comments are true.

Orvus Lee Houk, who claimed to be a relative of Jesse James, quoted Dalton as saying:

> "Charley [that's the way Houk spelled his name] Bigelow's gang of outlaws, who were deliberately parading about using my name -- Jesse James." P. 112 JJ AND THE LOST CAUSE

So if this is true, Charlie's use of the name Jesse James was creating additional problems for Dalton by masquerading as Jesse. This would increase the pressure on law enforcement to put an end to the real Jesse himself.

So this gives the ultimate motive for Dalton to remove Charlie Bigelow and his gang members. And it appears as if Dalton did just that. He reported that three men were shot that morning at the Bigelow home: Charlie and two of his brothers:

> ". . . I shot Bigelow and my Negro cook [meaning John Trammel, Jesse's friend and gang member] and I shot the other two bandits [named Bert and John by J. Frank Dalton, page 2 in JJ WAS ONE OF HIS NAMES] in that old barn behind the house." JJ AND THE LOST CAUSE, PAGE 12

61

Dalton added this additional comment:

"Three men died in the barn near that old Lafayette Street House [the Bigelow house in St. Joseph.] One we buried under my name. The other two dead bandits we smuggled out after dark that same night and disposed of." J J AND THE LOST CAUSE, p. 113

It is interesting to note that the "Frank Dalton" who was asked to write a chapter in the book entitled THE CRITTENDEN MEMOIRS by the son of the governor, claimed to be in the room where "Dalton" had brought the body of Bigelow after shooting him in the barn outside of the house. This is from page 363 of those MEMOIRS:

"I don't know why the real reason for the killing of Jesse James was never made public for Bob Ford told it to the Sheriff and others of us when we were in the room where Jesse lay dead."

The author Ted Yeatman gave the reader one clue in his book as to why Dalton, presuming he was the real Jesse James, wanted to remove Charlie Bigelow. He claimed it involved the bank robbery at Northfield, Minnesota, in 1876. This is the gang's bank robbery that failed miserably.

Mr. Yeatman wrote this:

"Cole [Younger] also said that the James brothers did not participate in the Northfield raid. It [the reported involvement of the James brothers] was a transparent lie; Cole insisted that the men involved were actually two other men named Woods and Howard."

So Cole was admitting that the Jesse and Frank DID NOT

participate in the bank robbery

But far more importantly, he identified the two men who did appear in the total of eight men (or possibly nine,) one of which was named "Howard" (obviously a last name,) the name that Charlie Bigelow assumed in St. Joseph, Missouri, while also living as Jesse James.

So maybe Cole was telling the truth in both statements, and one of the other robbers was "Howard," meaning Charlie Bigelow living under the name of Tom Howard.

So maybe Cole knew that "Howard" was Tom Bigelow.

I shall explain why this is significant in a later section when I discuss the entire Northfield raid.

This claim poses a real problem because J. Frank Dalton as Jesse James, claimed that he did participate in the robbery. If that is true, then Cole Younger was not telling the truth. One can speculate that Younger said what he said as a way of hopefully clearing his good friends Jesse and Frank from involvement in the robbery.

So, who did participate is still unclear.

But it is certainly possible that both Jesse AND Charlie Bigelow participated in he bank holdup.

One author claims that he has physical proof that Jesse James (meaning J. Frank Dalton) participated in the Northfield bank robbery on that day.

Henry J. Walker claims that he met with Mr. Dalton on August 9, 1949 and provided him with that evidence. Mr. Walker showed Mr. Dalton a watch that Walker claimed had been given to the inn-keeper in an inn near Northfield by Jesse James himself, apparently as payment for a room that he had rented before the Northfield bank robbery. Walker claimed he had obtained possession of the watch from a friend of his who got it from a safe belonging to the inn-keeper.

When Dalton was handed the watch, he recognized it and told Mr. Walker that it had been he who had traded it to the inn-keeper. Dalton later admitted that he and his brother Frank were the only two who had made a full escape from the Northfield robbery. (Pages 96-99 of Walker's book)

The bank robbery in Northfield did not go well. History has recorded that there were eight gang members in the robbery, and this is what happened to each of those men:

1. Jesse James
   Escaped after the robbery
2. Frank James
   Escaped but wounded during holdup
3. Cole Younger
   Captured after the bank robbery
4. James Younger
   Captured after the bank robbery, later committed suicide
5. Bob Younger
   Captured after the bank robbery
6. Clel Miller
   Shot dead at the site of the robbery
7. William Stiles
   Shot dead at the site of the robbery
8. Charles Pitts
   Shot dead in the capture of the Younger brothers

(There is some dispute about how many robbers there were in this gang that day. George Huntington's book entitled ROBBER AND HERO makes the claim three times that there were NINE and not eight robbers seen prior to the robbery. (Pages 1, 3, and 14) And he only lists eight by name, meaning that the name of this "ninth" gang member has never been found.

Now, assuming that Cole Younger was correct, that Jesse was not present at the robbery, then the question is who was the man that most historians claim was the real Jesse. Notice that Cole called the two men "Woods and Howard." Is it possible that this "Howard" was "Tom Howard," the man that the real Jesse shot in the barn outside of the house in St. Joseph?

Could this be a veiled reference to the fact that it was Charlie Bigelow who was part of the gang on this robbery, either as the unnamed "ninth man" or as one of the eight using the alias of Jesse James?

Is it possible that Charlie Bigelow went to the Northfield robbery as part of the gang but fled before the robbery started? Could it be that Bigelow had somehow informed the Pinkertons, or some other law enforcement authority, that Jesse and his gang were coming to rob the bank, and that was the reason the robbery went so poorly? Did the citizens have advance knowledge of the event because of Charlie Bigelow? Is it possible that this is the reason that writers have recorded that Jesse didn't trust Charlie? That Jesse felt he had betrayed him in Northfield?

Is it possible that "Tom Howard" was in truth Charlie Bigelow, living under that alias as Dalton claimed? Is it also possible that somehow "Howard" was claiming to be Jesse James at other times, and that is the reason that Dalton, the real Jesse James, killed him?

65

This would seem to fit the comments made by these individuals. It would also explain why Jesse felt he had to act, especially if he felt that "Howard" had endangered the safety of his gang by not properly assisting them in this robbery that finished with these disastrous results. Jesse would have acted out of sympathy for his friends, meaning the Younger family, and the others killed after the attempted robbery who he might have felt were betrayed by Bigelow.

These quotations when taken together have supplied the possible motive for the shooting of Charlie Bigelow by the real Jesse James: he had done two unforgivable things in outlaw terms:

1.   He had betrayed Jesse and all of the other gang members by infiltrating Jesse's gang and then revealing their plans to law enforcement officers, most likely the Pinkerton's Detective Agency. Jesse's "code of ethics" was that anyone betraying his cause had to pay the ultimate price for it: elimination.

2.   Charlie had organized his own gang and was using the name of Jesse as he was stealing and robbing. This could not be tolerated by Jesse so he had to remove not only Charlie but other members of the gang as well. If Dalton was correct, those other two men shot by Jesse and John Trammel must have been members of the Bigelow gang.

And that is exactly what Jesse James did on the morning of April 3, 1882.

It was certainly an added bonus when it occurred to Jesse that he could shoot Charlie and then claim that the dead man was the real Jesse James, and so he concocted the entire tale. And it worked.

After the scenario had played itself out, Jesse James could then continue living his life without the threat of the reward hanging over his head.

Jesse's plan would be an application of the proverbial "killing two birds with one stone."

1.   He could eliminate Charlie Bigelow for his treachery to him and his gang members, and

2.   He could kill off the name of Jesse James, and continue his life without too much fear of being discovered as the real Jesse James.

All of this evidence tends to support the conclusion that it was not the real "Jesse James that Bob Ford shot" in the house.

There is one more testimony that we must consider: the observation made by Zarelda James, Jesse's mother, when she saw the body of the man she was told was her son.

"Frank Dalton," the man who wrote the chapter in CRITTENDEN'S MEMOIRS, claimed that when Jesse's mother, Zarelda James Samuel, saw the body of "Jesse" after the shooting she stated that it was not her son. Dalton wrote:

> "Zarelda looked at the dead man and turning to the Sheriff and the others in the room, said: 'Gentlemen, you have made a mistake; that is not my son.'" (Page 364 MEMOIRS)

All of this tends to prove that the man shot that day was Charlie Bigelow, and not Jesse James.

Cole Younger, a member of Jesse's gang and certainly a

lifelong supporter of Jesse's, provided some evidence about one of the two motives for Dalton's claims about why he had decided to kill Charlie Bigelow: the decision to kill off the name of Jesse James.

> "Every daylight robbery in any part of the country, from the Alleghenies to the Rockies, was laid at our doors; we could not go out without a pair of pistols to protect ourselves from the attack of we knew not whom . . . ." (Page 161 JESSE JAMES THE MAN AND THE MYTH]

One can only imagine the fear that these men had when trying to live their lives on a day to day basis. This was the price of being a hunted outlaw: people wanted them removed so that they could lead a normal life without fear of their being robbed.

This certainly was a powerful motive for Jesse to kill off the name of Jesse James so that he would no longer be a hunted man. And this comment by Younger helps the reader understand that Dalton's comments are accurate.

So, according to Dalton/James, it was he, the real Jesse James, who shot Charlie as he entered the barn near his house early that morning on the Bigelow property in St. Joseph, Missouri. And it was he who claimed that he and several of his gang members carried the body of Mr. Bigelow into the house and laid it against a wall. It was he who claimed that he instructed Charlie's wife that she was to tell the sheriff when he appeared that the man on the floor was her husband, Jesse James, the famous outlaw, and that it was he who was living in the town under the alias of Tom Howard.

Mrs. Bigelow was further instructed to tell the sheriff that her name was Zerelda Mimms James, the name of the woman who many feel had married the real outlaw in 1874 and was known publicly as Jesse's wife. She was then told to tell her two children, a little boy of four and a girl of seven, that they were now to be called Jesse E. James and Mary James.

And Mrs. Bigelow did as she was told when the sheriff and others appeared. Her willingness to tell these lies was encouraged by $15,000 that Jesse gave her to tell them this lie, according to the book co-authored by Orvus Lee Houk and Del Schrader entitled JESSE JAMES WAS ONE OF HIS NAMES.

And history records that Mrs. Bigelow did as she had been told. The man on the floor was identified as "Jesse James," her husband, by "Mrs. Jesse Woodson James."

The following is an extremely thought provoking comment made by J. Frank Dalton in the book entitled JESSE JAMES AND THE LOST CAUSE: page 22

"It was Bigelow that had married Zarelda Mimms."

History has shown a picture of Zarelda Mimms James with her two children for years as the official picture (my research has found only one other picture of Zee Mimms besides this one) of Zarelda James. That same history has recorded that Zarelda (called Zee) married the real Jesse Woodson James, her first cousin, on April 24, 1874.

It is an interesting observation to make at this juncture that there has been "no public acknowledgment of Jesse's mother [Zarelda Cole James] having attended her son's wedding." Is it possible that the reason she did not is because Zee did not marry her son, but she married Charlie Bigelow? (JESSE

Since that picture of Zee and her two children was taken just days after the shooting of Jesse James in 1882, it must have been taken of the woman that Charlie Bigelow had married, if Dalton is correct, and not that of any of the women that the real Jesse James married.

So it would appear that the two children in that picture, called Jesse Edwards James and Mary Susan James, were in truth the two children of Mr. and Mrs. Bigelow and not those of Jesse James. There is certainly a possibility that Jesse had two children by that name, and forced Mrs. Bigelow to adopt those two names to give additional credibility to the entire story.

It would be appropriate now to examine one other possibility: that it was the real Jesse and his wife Zee living in the house in St. Joseph, Missouri and that they invited Charlie Bigelow to visit and it was then that Jesse shot him and dragged him into the living room. And that it was his real wife, the woman named Zee, that Jesse had tell the story to the sheriff.

This last scenario does not fit the facts, however, since the person known as Tom Howard (the name that Charlie Bigelow had been using as an alias in St. Joseph,) whoever he was, had been seen in St. Joseph by citizens of the city for months prior to the actual date of the shooting. The following are comments made about Jesse's visits in the city of St Joseph, Missouri, in the book entitled THE RISE AND FALL OF JESSE JAMES: (page 366)

"Mr. Howard [meaning Jesse using an alias,] the preceding winter [meaning the winter of 1881, just months before the shooting in April of 1882] had entertained the Ferrell girls at 1320 Lafayette Street, adjoining his home, by playing with them at snow-balling."

"Mr. Howard was a regular customer of August Bro-kaw, the druggist on lower Sixth street. He became a warm favorite there."

"It is positively known that Jesse James attended the Sunday services at the Presbyterian church . . . repeatedly. Last Sunday, he was seen with his entire family at the Union Depot, viewing the improvements."

Even Zee James added her comments about the presence of her husband in the city prior to the shooting. She was quoted as saying:

"We lived there nearly a year and Jesse went all over the town." (Page 95, THE LIFE AND TRAGIC TIMES OF JESSE JAMES by an anonymous writer)

The St. Joseph Weekly Gazette of April 5, 1882, added additional evidence that Jesse was a regular visitor to sites all over the city:

"Among other things told of Jesse, it was stated that Harry Carter, of the Missouri Valley Coal Company, got pretty well acquainted with Jesse, who bought all his fuel from this company . . . ." (Page 5)

This man had to be Charlie Bigelow if J. Frank Dalton is correct, because people in St. Joseph, when viewing the body of Jesse at the funeral, certainly would have been quick to point out that the man in the casket was not the man that they had repeatedly seen in their city posing as Mr. Howard, if it

71

was the real Jesse living in the St. Joseph home with his real wife Zee Mimms.

One clue that Zarelda Mimms James (actually Bigelow) knew little or nothing about the life of the real Jesse James is this comment from the book entitled THE LIFE AND TRAGIC DEATH OF JESSE JAMES (page 94) by an anonymous writer. He claims to have quoted the woman known as Zee James shortly after the shooting:

"There's one thing certain, what I do know of Jesse will never be made public.

I'll go to my grave without telling anything."

This reluctance on the part of Zee James to discuss her husband's past was confirmed by the book written by Stella F. James, the wife of Jesse Edwards James, the son of Charlie and Zee Bigelow. She stated this on page 29 of her book entitled IN THE SHADOW OF JESSE JAMES:

"Zee James did not talk to me of her life with Jesse James when he was a hunted man. She did talk a great deal about her children, about her hopes for Jesse, Jr."

She added an additional comment on page 35:

"I could not reconcile this gentle woman with Jesse James the bandit. To be perfectly truthful, I never have been able to do so."

There is one more clue that "Mrs. Jesse James" was not who she claimed to be. During the coroner's inquest into the death of the victim, Mrs. James was asked this question:

72

"Q: Where has he [meaning her husband, Jesse
        James] been at other times, can you tell?"

A: Yes, I could tell but I don't feel disposed to do
        so."

There was one other challenge to her memory of prior events
during this inquest and it came when the prosecutor asked her
this question:

"Q: Where is Frank ? [meaning Frank James, Jes-
        se's brother.]
A: I don't know.
Q: Is Frank living?
A: I don't know."

It seems rather difficult to understand how Jesse's wife would
not know whether or not Jesse's brother was still living, especially if the reports that he had been seen in St. Joseph during the days around the shooting. One would expect that
brother Frank would have wanted to visit his brother Jesse if
both were in the same town at the same time. And if they met,
it would be presumed that Zee would have seen them together.

Of course, if her husband was not the real Jesse, it is conceivable that she would not have known whether or not Frank
James was alive, nor would she have been able to identify
him out of a crowd.

There are two explanations as to why the "gentlewoman" Zee
did not talk about Jesse James, the outlaw:

1.   She chose not to just because she chose not to.
        She certainly had this right and could have

simply chosen not to discuss their lives together before the shooting.

2. She did not know much about the life of the real Jesse James prior to the shooting, having been only the wife of Charlie Bigelow, and not the wife of the real outlaw. This would be the logical belief if she had been forced to accept the identity of Zee James by the threat of violence to her from the real Jesse James.

But this then poses an additional problem.

The James family Bible has the following listing in it regarding Zee Mimms James: (her's is the 12th name of the 16 listed) and it seems unlikely that the James family would put her name in their family Bible if she was not married to Jesse Woodson James. That is, unless Zarelda James, the real mother of Jesse James, put it in there to further conceal the fact that she knew that it was Charlie Bigelow that was shot as the real Jesse James, and that it was his wife that had to be passed off as Zee Mimms, the wife of the real Jesse. She would have had to put her name in the Bible as further evidence that Zee and the real Jesse were married.

To further lend support to the fact that the name of Zee Mimms was added after the date of the shooting in 1882, it is listed as follows:

"Zarelda Mimmbs [the spelling in the Bible](James)
born -- ? --, 1845
died November 30, 1900."

So whoever wrote this into the Bible did not know the birthdate of Zarelda Mimmbs, so they left it blank.

74

So the Bible offers no assistance to the researcher: was this Zarelda Mimmbs Bigelow or Zarelda Mimmbs James?

(I have often said that this Jesse James story is like walking in a fog with blinders on! It is that confusing.)

But, notwithstanding all of this, I believe that it was Charlie Bigelow and his wife and two children who were living in St. Joseph, Missouri as the wife and family of "Jesse James." And that it was not the real Jesse Woodson James and his wife Zee Mimms James in that house.

There is another clue that the Bigelow family was the one living in the house when the shooting took place.

This comes from the book entitled THE RISE AND FALL OF JESSE JAMES by Robertus Love when he discussed the two children of "Jesse and Zee James": (page 278)

"Two children came, Jesse Edwards and Mary.

But young Jesse never knew his own name -- first, middle or last -- until he was nearly seven years of age and the fatal bullet made him fatherless and relieved the little family of further necessity for concealment of identity.

His father always called him Tim; to his mother he was Eddie."

This explanation that they had to conceal their identities if they were the real Jesse James family certainly could be true, because Jesse would have wanted to protect them, but it is also possible that these were the real names of the son of Charlie and Zee Bigelow. And that the name of Jesse Edward was forced upon him by the order of the real Jesse James, under penalty of death.

Once again, this is just a clue and not concrete evidence. But it does lend some credibility to the Dalton scenario: the Bigelow male child was never called Jesse Edwards until after the shooting.

But the reason Jesse James was conducting this enormous fraud was because he had decided that it was time to kill off the name of Jesse James, because there were too many individuals, including bounty hunters, who were interested in either the reward money, which was substantial in those days, or the honor of being "the man who killed Jesse James." So Jesse realized that his future was in danger.

After the shooting of Charlie Bigelow, the body was removed to the funeral parlor in St. Joseph. The sheriff sent a telegram to Zarelda James, known publicly as the mother of Jesse James, in Kearney, Missouri, about 30 miles away, asking her to come to St. Joseph to identify the body as being that of her son, Jesse Woodson James.(There is some dispute as to who sent the telegram. Others say it was the lady living in the house with the deceased, the woman called Zarelda Mimms James.

In fact, she testified in the Coroner's Inquest that it was her who had asked a Doctor to send the telegram. She further explained that she did not write the telegram, but that she just told him where to send it.) (ST. JOSEPH DAILY GAZETTE, April 5, 1882, front page)

But, as I already mentioned, when she arrived in St. Joseph and viewed the body of the man on the funeral director's tabe, history has recorded that she correctly proclaimed that the body was NOT that of her son, Jesse Woodson James. If Mr. Dalton is right, she was telling the truth, because it was the body of Charlie Bigelow, and her denial has puzzled James historians for a long time. Since this is part of the recorded history of the day, the fact that she stated that the man on the table was not her son is a real problem to those who believe that the real Jesse was shot that day in St. Joseph.

But Dalton's claim was that one of his friends took her aside after her denial and explained to her that she had to agree that Charlie Bigelow was her son so that Jesse could continue living. And that is what she did. Mr. Houk in his book mentioned that her decision was encouraged by a thousand dollar bill given to her by Dalton (Jesse) himself.

She must have pondered that request for a few minutes, because it was asking her to lie to a sheriff. But, after reflecting upon the reasons as stated by Jesse's friends, she went back into the room and made the claim that she had been mistaken, that the body was that of her son Jesse James. She then tried to explain why she had changed her story. She claimed that it had been some time since she had seen her son and secondly, the beard that the dead man wore confused her because it was not often that her son Jesse had worn a beard.

Frank Triplett in his book entitled THE LIFE, TIMES AND TREACHEROUS DEATH OF JESSE JAMES reports further evidence that Zarelda was lying about the identity of "Jesse James," meaning the man on the table. He reported on page 224 of his book that Jesse had seen his mother just a few days before the shooting. He had been:

". . . visiting his mother at her home, in Clay County, on Friday, two weeks before he was killed . . . ."

This visit of Jesse to the home of his mother was also covered in Marley Brant's book entitled JESSE JAMES: THE MAN AND THE MYTH: (page 223)

> "Jesse visited his mother and her family in Clay County at the end of March 1882."

So, if this story is correct, as it appears to be, Zarelda could not have claimed she hadn't seen Jesse for several years and that she could not recognize him with his beard.

It might be important to examine why the sheriff was depending on the testimony of these two women and others who claimed to know Jesse James before the shooting.

Various writers of the James story have shown reproductions of the wanted posters for the James brothers and none of them have any pictures or drawings of the two outlaws. And that had to be because the authorities had no photographs or drawings of the brothers to be used on their posters.

One author who spoke to this question was Michael Fellman, who wrote the introduction to Robertus Love's book entitled THE RISE AND FALL OF JESSE JAMES. This is what he wrote:

> "The James [brothers] . . . made sure that no photographs of themselves came to light to help the detectives [and obviously other legal authorities] hunting them."

As a possible evidence that Dalton is right, Cole Younger, a member of Jesse's gang, gave an interview that was published in Carl Briehan's book (page 151) after Cole's death. He responded to this question:

Q: "Was Jesse James killed at St. Joe as was claimed?"

A: "He certainly was. We Youngers [Cole had several brothers, at least three of whom were members of Jesse's gang] were shown photos of the dead man, and we knew it was Jesse . . . ."

If Dalton is correct that the man in the photographs was Charlie Bigelow, Cole Younger and his brothers lied as well. They certainly would have wanted to protect their leader and apparently they did so by providing the authorities with reinforcement of Jesse's phony story.

Mr. Dalton claimed that he stayed around the St. Joseph area for several days after he had murdered Charlie Bigelow, and actually attended his own funeral. He claimed that he had a piece of metal created that he could fit into his mouth to change his outward appearance. Under this new look, he attended his own funeral, sang in the choir, and later helped carry his own casket.

The possibility that Jesse helped carry his own casket was discussed by this report of the two writers Phillip W. Steele and George Warfel in their book entitled THE MANY FACES OF JESSE JAMES: (page 64)

"The pallbearers were J.D. Ford, Charles Scott, James Henderson, J.T. Reed, and William Bond.

A sixth pallbearer, who no one seemed to know, was 'Jim Vaughn.'

The true identity of that sixth pallbearer still remains

a mystery."

Frank Triplett adds a few more details about this mysterious pallbearer in his book: (page 281):

> "The Sixth was a man whom no one had seen until just as the procession was about to start; he then came forward, his countenance stern, his eye bright and piercing. Moving to the head of the casket he directed the movements of the others quietly, dumbly, yet with a mien sad and commanding.
>
> His apparent age was about forty years [Jesse James was born in 1847, and would have been 35 at the time of the funeral] but his lithe, muscular figure seemed to deny such age . . . .
>
> None seemed to know him; none questioned him, and he spoke to no one. Who was he? Where was he from? Was it Frank James?"

Close, but no cigar!

Once again, these stories confirm that very few knew what Jesse and his brother looked like because of their efforts to keep photographs of them out of circulation.

If Dalton's story is correct, then Jim Vaughn was in truth Jesse James, appearing at his own funeral!

One who confirmed that Jesse James once used the alias of Vaughn was Jesse James Benton. Mr. Benton claims that he met both Jesse and Frank James while his family ranched in "Denton County in the north-middle of Texas."

Mr. Benton was born in 1864 and his family moved to Texas sometime in the year of 1872. He made these observations in his book entitled COW BY THE TAIL:

"The next bunch of outlaws to visit our place were Frank and Jesse James who have been friends of my father back in Kentucky. I have been named after Jesse James.

Frank and Jesse visited our place about twice a year. We children did not know anything about their being bandits, as they went by the name of the Vaughn brothers." (Page 28)

Confirmation of Mr. Benton's claim is found on page 8 of the book entitled JESSE JAMES WAS ONE OF HIS NAMES in the list of the 72 aliases that Jesse assumed. They are in alphaetical order and near the end of that list is the name:

Tom Vaughn.

This certainly wasn't the same name that the authors claim was the name of the mysterious 6th pallbearer, but it is some confirmation that Jesse used an alias similar to that in his past.

But before I introduce other material, I must ask why it was of so much importance to these authors? Who cared who this 6th pallbearer was? Why waste the time asking the question?

Is it possible that they were offering their readers one clue that they knew who this mysterious pallbearer was and they were secing if the readers would see that on their own?

It certainly could have been J. Frank Dalton who claimed to have helped carry his own casket at the funeral!

Dalton used to claim: "I know I am dead, because I saw them bury me." (JESSE JAMES RIDES AGAIN, page 7)

One of the stranger events in the funeral of Jesse James was this ending statement by Rev. J.M.P. Martin at the request by Zarelda James, according to Mr. Triplett (page 283):

> "Before the coffin is taken from the house I have been asked to make one or two requests.
>
> As John Samuel [Jesse's half-brother] is very low on account of the shock caused by the death of his brother, and as the grave is very near the house [at the James farm, about 4 miles outside of Kearney] Mrs. Samuel asks that those who are here will not go out to the house. It is feared that the excitement of seeing so many persons will injure him. It is therefore requested that no one but the friends and relatives go to the grave."

Apparently this was done, and the body of Jesse was taken to the farm and laid in a grave near the house.

But for the purists, this means that there were no independent witnesses to the burial itself, so no one can be certain that the body of Jesse was laid in that grave on the farm.

Several photographs have been preserved of Zarelda Samuels, Jesse's mother, standing by the grave in her side yard, with a huge gravestone in the shape of an obelisk, that was taller than she was, besides her. This would imply that the family did not want anyone to miss the fact that this was the site where Jesse was buried. These photographs might have been taken to record for posterity that this was the location of the James body, for reasons I will discuss in a few paragraphs.

Vandals chipped away at that stone tombstone over the years to the point where only a small portion of it remains even today (it was found many years after the funeral and is currently on display at the James Farm museum.)

What I am wondering is how does anyone know for certain that the James family buried the body of "Jesse" at this site near the house? No one but the "friends and relatives" had seen the burial and the pictures of Zarelda standing by the obelisk must have taken to convince the world that Jesse was indeed buried at the James farm., and at this precise location.

There certainly could be a possibility that they buried another body in that grave, and buried the body of Charlie Bigelow somewhere else on the farm. If a Bigelow had come to the farm to dig up the body to prove that it was his family member buried there, the James family could have claimed that they buried another body under the obelisk and buried the "James" body elsewhere to protect it from grave robbers. And that this was done to protect the James family from knowledge that their relative's burial spot had been tampered with.

But it is the truth that no independent party saw the casket containing the body of "Jesse James" buried in the plot besides the James house on the farm grounds. The closing comments made by the minister prove that.

One additional clue that the body buried on the James farm was not even that of Charlie Bigelow is this one, provided by Robertus Love in his book entitled THE RISE AND FALL OF JESSE JAMES (page 373):

> "Disinternment of the remains this morning [meaning June 29, 1902] revealed the fact that somebody --
> either the great state of Missouri or an undertaker --

had deceived the James family at the first burial twenty years ago [meaning the burial in 1882.]

It was represented at that time that the coffin in which the body was shipped from St. Joseph [in 1882] was in an enduring metallic casket, costing $500, and that the body had been embalmed.

When the old coffin was lifted out of the grave it fell apart, and there was nothing inside but the skeleton in clothing."

So the casket that carried the body of Jesse James to his family's farm was metal, but the casket dug up by his family in 1902 to move it to the cemetery was wood. That means that the casket buried in the site near the house was not the casket carried there after the funeral.

The inferences of these facts are staggering: what happened to the metal casket that supposedly bore the body of "Jesse" to his family's farm?

No author that I know of has tackled this question.

However, it is known that when the body was removed from the grave in 1902, it was placed in a metal casket. That was confirmed by Mr. Yeatman in his book:

"It had been reported in 1902 that Jesse's remains were reburied in a metal coffin . . . ." (Page 336)

This second metal casket will play a significant role in the DNA tests conducted in 1988 during the exhumation of the James body, and that fact will be discussed later in this book for very important reasons.

There is one additional clue, already discussed in another context, that the man shot in St. Joseph was not Jesse James, and that was the fact that many observers of the time expected Frank James to avenge the death of his brother by killing Bob Ford, as has been already discussed in this book.

Yet Frank never did this, and one can only wonder why. Is it possible that Frank was nearby during the events surrounding the death of Jesse, and that he too knew that Bob Ford did not shoot his brother? It would seem to be a reasonable conclusion that he did because he took no revenge on Bob Ford after the shooting. (I previously quoted the comment that Frank and Bob were seen together after the shooting.)

But I have found no evidence that Frank ever commented on this, so history will probably never know.

chapter six
CHARLIE BIGELOW AND
HIS TWO DEAD RELATIVES

As I have mentioned, J. Frank Dalton claimed that he shot a fellow gang member known as Charlie Bigelow in St. Joseph on the morning of April 2, 1882.

There are many historians who claim that they can find no record of a Charlie Bigelow in any listing made of the known member of Jesse's gang. I would have to agree with them by stating that I have found no such name in any listing I have found in my research.

However, the television program called IN SEARCH OF interviewed John Nicholson, a grand nephew of Jesse James, and he stated that he knew where two **Bigelow** brothers were buried. The television crews accompanied Mr. Nicholson as he visited "the old Haynesville cemetery by Holt, Missouri" where he knew the two **Bigelows** were buried. The program's cameras panned down to show the two graves in the grass of this old cemetery (the two tombstones have fallen over and were laying flat in the grass.)

The two tombstones read as follows:

1.   Name on tombstone:
      JOHN G. BIGELOW
      Died: June 25, 1864
      Aged 41 years (it is difficult to read because
      the tombstone is weathering with age, but it
      appears to then say 2 months and 20 days)

There is clearly a MASONIC square and compass on the top quarter of the tombstone, meaning that **John G. Bigelow** was a member of the Masons

2.   Name on tombstone:
      SALMON G. BIGELOW (The first name appears to be Salmon, but it also has weathered with age, and is hard to read) Died: June 25, 1864
      Aged 43 years, (once again, weathering has reduced the ability to read the letters but it appears to then say 2 months and 17 days)

And just as on the tombstone of **JOHN G. BIGELOW**, there is clearly a MASONIC square and compass on the top quarter of the tombstone, meaning that **Salmon G. Bigelow** was also a member of the Masonic Lodge

I must admit that it is difficult to make out the first name of this Bigelow. It appears to be **SALMON** (not Samuel, nor Solomon, nor Simeon.).

One writer, Ted Yeatman, found the James-Bigelow connection and wrote about it in his book entitled JESSE AND FRANK: (page 51):

"There would be numerous collisions with the Federals that summer. Jesse James was probably present at the siege of the home of militiamen **Simeon** and **John Bigelow** during the last week in June [of 1864.] Both Bigelows were killed after a desperate fight."

Notice that Mr. Yeatman has the name of one of the brothers as Simeon. However, this is not correct. The name on the tombstone could not be Simeon, because the letter M is clearly the fourth letter, not the third. The best I can do with the name is Salmon.

Notice that Mr. Yeatman states that the two brothers were "militiamen" when they were shot only about a year after some members of the "Missouri militia came to the James-Samuel farm in May 1863."

Mr. Yeatman does not connect the two incidents, the shooting of the two **Bigelows** and the incident when Jesse and his step father were questioned about the whereabouts of Frank James by troops in Northern uniforms during the Civil War.

But the evidence he presents indicates that the events are connected.

I found the "town" of Holt, Missouri, near Haynesville on a map of Missouri and both cities are about 10 miles north of Kearney, Missouri. Neither city is listed in the Rand McNally Road Atlas of 1994, but the computer website known as MAPQUEST.COM located them and showed them on their map. So it appears as if both cities exist or existed at one time. And it is certain that the cemetery exists because the television program shot film of the two tombstones when they visited it with their cameras.

Mr. Nicholson claimed that the two men were brothers, but there is no confirmation of that fact on the two tombstones, and I have not found the reason he would have made that statement. The evidence tends to fit his opinion, but the conclusion that they were brothers cannot be made from the on-site evidence.

Marley Brant, one writer on the story of Jesse James, offered this tantalizing bit of evidence in his book JESSE JAMES

THE MAN AND THE MYTH on pages 272 - 273:

> "[Jesse's] finger tip probably was lost in June of 1864 in a battle in which two Clay Countians named Bigelow were killed by the Jameses and others who were commanded by Fletcher Taylor."

So, Mr. Brant does not say that they were brothers, but at least he is of the opinion that the two Bigelows were murdered by Jesse and others in the right year.

Dalton claimed that he had shot two more Bigelows, for a grand total of five (the two in 1864, two in 1882, and Charlie.) There is additional support for the idea that there were other members of the James gang at the time of the Charlie Bigelow shooting in 1882, possibly meaning two or more brothers of Charlie Bigelow, around the St. Joseph area. This quotation comes from THE ENCYCLOPEDIA OF WESTERN GUNFIGHTERS (page 170) under the name of JAMES, JESSE WOODSON:

> "April 3, 1882, St. Joseph, Missouri: For the past several months Jesse, under the name of Thomas Howard, had been living with his family AND SEVERAL COHORTS in St. Joseph." (Emphasis by Epperson)

But, unfortunately for history, these "cohorts" were unnamed by this source. So it still conceivable that the COHORTS of Charlie Bigelow could have been his two brothers, and possibly others, just as Mr. Dalton claimed.

Now there are only three possibilities as I see it as to who these two Bigelow men shot in 1864 might have been:

1.   They were individuals, possibly brothers, with

no known connection to the James story. This is certainly possible, and cannot be dismissed.

However, there are some problems with that position.

Mr. Nicholson, who took the IN SEARCH OF television crew to the cemetery where the Bigelows were buried, said his grandfather told him that these were the two Bigelows shot by Jesse James, so we must at least examine that possibility.

2.   They were the brothers of Charlie Bigelow. But this poses a difficult problem for Dalton's position that he killed both of them in 1882.

Both tombstones show that the men were killed on the same day like Dalton claimed, but they were killed in 1864, not 1882. It would be extremely difficult to develop a scenario where they could have been buried in 1882 with tombstones showing that their deaths occurred in 1864.

So it would seem unlikely that Dalton killed them (if these are the same two brothers) in 1882 in St. Joseph, Missouri and then rigged the date of their death on their tombstones to read 1864. It would seem nearly impossible to convince the friends and family of the deceased to allow them to make these changes in the date of their death.

And if they were the two brothers that Jesse claimed to have shot, why do the two tombstones say they were shot back in 1864? That year was in the latter years of the Civil War, (1861 - 1865) when Jesse was reported to have been riding with **Quantrill**'s Raiders.

Were these two "brothers" assisting the North during these years of the Civil War?

There could be a way that they were both involved with Jesse James back in 1863.

Could they have been involved with the hangings of both Jesse and his stepfather on the James farm in Kearney during the questioning by some Union soldiers about Frank's whereabouts? They were both buried near Kearney, so it could be conceivable that they were two Missouri brothers who had joined the Northern cause not favored by the James family.

If this is true, then it could be conceivable that Jesse killed both of them as being "Missouri traitors" to the cause of the South, and he was taking revenge for their involvement in the hanging of his stepfather and for the burning of his feet during that interrogation about Frank's whereabouts, in the episode of 1863. Jesse could have searched for them and killed both of them when he found them, for their handling of the interrogation.

But I have not found any researcher who has directly identified a motive for Jesse shooting them back in 1864.

So, I must conclude that Jesse shot FOUR BIGELOWS, (actually FIVE, if you count Charlie:) TWO in 1864 and TWO in 1882.

3.   One of them was the father of Charlie Bigelow, the man Dalton claimed he shot in 1882 in the St. Joseph shooting.

According to the tombstones, these two Bigelows died in 1864 when they were 43 and 41. The latest date that Charlie could have been born if he was a son of one of the two men, would have to have been 1865, presuming that he was conceived at the latest date just before his father died.

However, the pictures of the dead man identified as Jesse James in the shooting of 1882 would seem to indicate that he was in his middle to late 30's, the same age as Jesse Woodson James would have been, age 35, in 1882. That means that he would have had to been born in 1847 or so, and he would have had to be approximately 17 when his father died.

If Charlie was a son of one of the two Bigelows shot in 1864, it could be inferred from the 1864 date that Charlie learned about his father's death at the hands of Jesse James and decided to kill the murderer of his father when he got close enough to do so.

Then it would have taken him as many as 18 years to find Jesse James and worm his way into his graces (Dalton claimed that Charlie was a "gang member") so as to be able to kill him before Jesse James discovered the reason he had joined his gang. It must be assumed that Charlie would not want Jesse to learn his real name, and this would account for the fact that no historian has ever learned that Charlie Bigelow was a member of the James gang. It is certainly conceivable that Charlie would have used an alias so as not to tip off Jesse that he was related to the two Bigelows that Jesse claimed he had shot in 1864.

From the claim that Bigelow couldn't be trusted, it can be inferred that Jesse must have discovered that Charlie was not about to shoot him himself, but to turn him in to the authorities looking for him, possibly for the reward money.

It could only be further presumed that Jesse must have learned of Charlie's purpose when he started noticing that Charlie could not be trusted with gang information. Jesse would have then taken steps to remove him because of his penchant for releasing information to the authorities about the locations and activities of Jesse's gang. Jesse could have also discovered his intention to murder him in 1882. Since Dalton identified him as Charlie Bigelow, it follows that he must have learned of Charlie's mission to kill the man who killed his father, and decided for that reason alone, he would have to be eliminated.

This seems to be the more reasonable explanation as to why no historian has ever been able to find the name of Charlie Bigelow in any listing of members of Jesse's gang.

And it seems to fit the evidence as far as it has appeared, but once again, it can only be the result of speculation, because the record is not clear.

In any event, Dalton claimed he shot Charlie Bigelow in St. Joseph, Missouri on April 3, 1882.

And from what we know of the situation, it seems to follow that that statement is true.

Jesse shot Charlie Bigelow before Charlie could either murder him or totally betray him.

And as a bonus, he was able to continue his life without too much fear because .... JESSE JAMES WAS DEAD!

chapter seven
REPORTS THAT
JESSE LIVED ON

Those who claim that the real Jesse James was shot in St. Joseph, Missouri have to deal with reports that he was seen alive after the day of the shooting. For instance, the story that follows is one such story from just days after the shooting that someone knew that J. Frank Dalton's version of his story was true.

There was a testimony of a neighbor in St. Joseph, Missouri, who claimed that he knew that Charlie Bigelow was going to be shot in 1882, and that in fact, he had been told this by:

> "a certain member of the James gang [who] had previously told me [meaning the resident] that this shooting was to take place."

This is that statement as recorded on page 12 of Rudy Turilli's booklet entitled THE TRUTH ABOUT JESSE JAMES:

> [this is Rudy telling the story:] "We found a man by the name of John Pierce, 95 years old. He revealed to us that he positively knew that Jesse James was not killed on April 3, 1882.
>
> He said that he had known the day before that a man by the name of Charlie Bigelow was going to be killed.
>
> He said he had been laying a stone fence two blocks

away on the morning of April 3, 1882, when he heard the shot.

He identified the [dead] man, known to him, as Charlie Bigelow. [Apparently he knew that the Howard name was an alias.] He also stated that he had seen Jesse James [alive] a few hours later."

Mr. Pierce went on to comment on the fatal shot to the back of Jesse's head and the lack of any evidence that the victim's face had been severely damaged from this shot to the rear of the victim's head:

"I would like to go back to the supposed killing of Jesse James on April 3, 1882. They tell us that a young fellow by the name of Robert Ford killed Jesse James with a .45 Colt revolver at a four foot distance. [Mr. Pierce's recollections are at variance with the official story that Bob Ford shoot Jesse with a .44 Smith & Wesson pistol.]

I am sure that if anyone is acquainted with a .45 caliber gun, he knows that if a man were shot at a four-foot distance with that type of gun, he would have a hole in his head as big as a baseball."

So here was one witness who challenged the official version of the story, but his comments went unheeded by the media and the governmental authorities examining the shooting.

Prior to the shooting of Bigelow, Jesse visited **Thomas T. Crittenden**, the Governor of Missouri (1881-1885), who was a boyhood friend of his while he (Jesse) was growing up with his family in Kentucky. Many years later, in 1880, when he was an adult, he had given Mr. **Crittenden** a campaign contribution of $70,000 to help finance his election bid. And now, two years later, Jesse must have felt that **the Governor** owed him a favor in return.

So Jesse met with him after the election and told him of his plans to kill off the name of Jesse James. He gave **the Governor** $10,000 to offer as reward money for the man who would shoot Jesse James.

This would be the point where I should add some additional evidence that Jesse James knew **the Governor** and that **the Governor** knew that Dalton was indeed the legendary outlaw.

In 1936, Henry Huston Crittenden, the son of **the Governor**, published a book entitled THE CRITTENDEN MEMOIRS, meaning a collection of his father's papers and recollections. Inside that book are 20 pages (pages 355 - 374) written by "Frank Dalton" at the request of the author inside a chapter entitled OUTLAWRY IN MISSOURI.

Henry Crittenden wrote this as an introduction to those 20 pages:

> "Frank Dalton, now living in Texas, who rode with **Quantrill** and the 'James boys' in the 70s as one of the band, gives pen pictures of the Missouri Outlaws. He visited old haunts in his native State, Missouri, in February, 1935, and appeared quite active in spite of his 87 years."

Just for a point of clarification, J. Frank Dalton, if he is the "Frank Dalton" who wrote these pages, would have been 87 years old in February of 1935 when the book came out. It might be recalled that Jesse Woodson James was born in 1847, making him 87 or 88 years old in 1935. That seems to imply that "Frank Dalton" was indeed Jesse James himself.

The chapter continues:

> "Though previously unknown to the writer, [apparently meaning Henry Crittenden] he [apparently meaning Dalton] called at the office to see my brother, Thomas T. Crittenden Jr., entirely unaware a history of the activities of the James gang and other outlaws was being compiled by the writer [apparently meaning Dalton was unaware that Crittenden was writing the book.]
>
> The following letters written by Frank Dalton for a Texas publication will no doubt prove interesting to the general public which is at all familiar with the terror created by the Missouri Outlaws. H.H.C. [obviously meaning Henry Huston Crittenden.]"

So it appears as if the two Crittenden brothers knew that "Frank Dalton" was the real Jesse James just like their father did. It must also be understood that if Jesse and the father were schoolmates in their early childhood in Kentucky, Jesse certainly would have known things that would prove to any Crittenden of that generation that he had grown up with **Thomas**, their father.

So when he contacted the two Crittenden brothers, they could substantiate that he was the early childhood friend of their father even if they didn't know that already. And that the two brothers felt that if anyone could write an accurate history about Jesse James, it would be Jesse James himself.

Now back to James story in St. Joseph, Missouri.

It has been recorded that the Ford brothers, the two assailants of Jesse James, never received the reward money (or perhaps only an amount as small as $250 each) and it is nearly impossible to know today where that money went. Some historians claim that it was divided up amongst the other individuals in the plot to shoot Jesse James, meaning the governor, the sheriff and the others.

One possible clue that this might be true was offered in the book THE RISE AND FALL OF JESSE JAMES (page 361). The author discussed a meeting that Zarelda James, the mother of Jesse, had with Bob Ford about three years after the 1882 shooting:

> "Ford also told Mrs. Samuel that he and his brother got only a few hundred dollars of the $10,000 reward. The rest appears to have been divided between some of the officials who connived the conspiracy."

(Notice that this was a meeting of the man who shot Jesse James and the mother of the man he had shot. The recorded conversation does not sound very bitter, nor did Zarelda seek any revenge on the murderer of her son! But it is far more interesting to note that Mr. Love, the author, made no comment about the fact that Mrs. James made no attempt to avenge the death of her son against the man history has recorded as being that "dirty little coward." He recorded the conversation almost as if it was being held amongst friends.)

Also, the reward was not for $10,000, according to the author (page 351): it was:

> "$5,000 for the apprehension of the outlaw, and $5,000 for his conviction in any court."

The house where Jesse was allegedly shot is currently a museum in St. Joseph, Missouri. Those who visit the home today are shown the hole in the wall where the bullet that struck Jesse went after it exited his head. The St. Joseph newspaper (page 5) of April 5, 1882, contained an article from "a Gazette reporter" who stated that he had seen "the hole left by the fatal bullet." That means that the hole was there the day of the shooting, or at the very least was placed there the very next day.

Since Bob Ford said that the bullet did not exit the body, then someone else put the bullet hole there, and that seems to fit the scenario of J. Frank Dalton. So, if Mr. Dalton is correct, that bullet hole was created after the actual shooting of Charlie Bigelow outside of the house.

Those who believe the bullet did not exit the body cannot rely on the inspection done of the body of Jesse James in 1995. Dr. James Starrs, the law and forensics professor at George Washington University who conducted the exhumation, stated on February 23, 1996 when he gave his review of the testing done on the body:

> "It goes back to the question of whether or not there was or was not an exit wound. I am not going to come forward and say exactly and precisely with any degree of even lesser than apodictive [defined as absolutely certain] certainty that there was no exit wound. We are dealing with -- we didn't have the full skeletal remains from the skull." (Yeatman, page 373)

Dr. Starrs then handed the question to Dr. Mike Finegan who was also present during the conference. Dr. Finegan then added his comments:

"So we can't be positive that there wasn't an exit wound, but certainly there was not an exit wound based on where the exit wound should have been once we analyzed the entrance wound." (Yeatman, page 373)

In fact, this conclusion is corroborated by the autopsy performed on the body of Jesse James in 1882, or the body of Charlie Bigelow, if Mr. Dalton is correct.

Marley Brant in his book entitled JESSE JAMES, THE MAN AND THE MYTH (page 229) reported this:

"An autopsy was performed . . . . It was confirmed that the bullet entered the occipital bone immediately behind the right ear and traveled upward. The bullet remained embedded in the skull behind the left ear."

It is obvious that if the bullet had remained in the skull, it certainly could not have exited the head and left that bullet hole in the wall in the James home, especially if Bob Ford claimed he only fired once.

Bob Ford answered that question in the Coroner's Inquest. He was handed the gun he supposedly used in the shooting and was asked:

"Q: How many balls were fired out of it?
A: One." DAILY GAZETTE, page 4

Dalton himself reported that he was very specific as to where he had shot Charlie Bigelow. He explained:

"Charlie Bigelow . . . was shot right over the right eye
. . . ." JJ AND THE LOST CAUSE p. 134

(There seems to be a dispute as to just where this shot hit Charlie. Here Dalton says it was over "the right eye" but the pictures of Bigelow after the shooting show him with only one injury on his face, and that is over his left eye. I guess it is possible that the picture was reversed, but this is highly unlikely since other photographs taken at the same time show the injury above his left eye. There was also testimony from those at the scene that they had seen a wound above the left eye. I guess it would be possible to say it was over his right eye, meaning the eye on the right side as viewed by Dalton.)

Of course, it is conceivable that Dalton was incorrect about exactly where he had shot Charlie, or he simply made a mistake in his recollections of an event that had taken place at least 66 years before.)

So Dalton's claim that he shot Charlie Bigelow above the right eyebrow seems to support the physical evidence but only IF the picture was reversed during developing. Because there were a series of photographs taken of Charlie Bigelow after he was examined by the legal authorities of St. Joseph, Missouri. But those pictures show his face intact other than what appears to be a small bullet hole over his left eyebrow. There is no apparent injury to the man's head above or near the right eye.

So this would have had to be an exit wound, if the story told by Bob Ford is correct. But it would have had to be an entrance wound if the story of Dalton is correct.

The St. Joseph Gazette's article on the shooting the day after the event reported:

"The ball [meaning the bullet] had entered the base of the skull and made its way out through the forehead

101

over the left eye."

That should clear up the matter of where this bullet exited the body. This report was made from the reporter's observations of the wound itself, when the reporter viewed the body. Clearly, the bullet exited over the LEFT eye according to the scenario believed by those who believe Jesse James was shot that day.

If, as is claimed, Jesse was shot in the rear of the head and the bullet exited through the front, it is presumed that the bullet would have done far more damage to Jesse's forehead than the evidence shows. In other words, Bigelow would have had a gaping hole over his left eye.

The reason for this can be explained: it is known that the bullets used during these days were rather soft, and that upon striking bones, they were often flattened which means they would have left enormous damage as they exited the body. That means that a small hole in the back and quite likely a large hole in the front would be the physical evidence on Bigelow's head after a fatal head shot from the rear. Yet the pictures taken after his death show his face intact, with the exception of a small injury above his left eye.

It is far more likely that the small hole in the front of his head was an entrance wound, because Dalton claimed that he shot Charlie Bigelow as he entered the barn that Jesse was hiding in. That means that Dalton claimed that he shot him in the face.

And this is what the evidence shows in the case of Charlie Bigelow. Pictures of him after his death show his head with but a small wound over his left eyebrow. But because he is laying on the table on his back, there is no way that the observer can determine whether or not there was a wound in the back of his head.

However, there is a report of the wounds in "Jesse's" head in a book entitled THE COMPLETE AND AUTHENTIC LIFE OF JESSE JAMES, written by Carl W. Breihan, (page 183) not a believer in the "J. Frank Dalton is Jesse James" theory. He wrote:

"Most accounts of the shooting say that the bullet entered the base of Jesse's skull at the back of his head and emerged over the left eye, [this means that the pictures of Jesse WERE NOT REVERSED, because Mr. Breihan says it was over his LEFT eye, just as the photographs reveal] lending credence to the belief that he was shot while his back was fully turned.

Re-examination of the testimony given at the inquest, however, indicates that the hole in Jesse's forehead was a clean wound, while the hole in the back of the head was ragged. The entrance hole of a bullet is generally clean; the exit less so. [This says that the body was shot in the front and experienced a larger hole in the back of the head as the bullet exited.]

This tends to substantiate Bob Ford's testimony that Jesse had started to turn around and face him when the shot was fired."

It also "tends to substantiate" the claim made by J. Frank Dalton as well.

This report seems to confirm the report that was made in 1902 when the body of the alleged Jesse was moved from the James farm to the cemetery in Kearney.

This is how Robertus Love described the event in his book
THE RISE AND FALL OF JESSE JAMES: (pages 375-376)

"As the coffin bottom was being turned around above
the ground, the skull again fell off and dropped to the
bottom of the grave.

At this juncture John Samuel [the half-brother to Jesse
James, meaning he was a son of Zarelda James and
her husband Dr. Reuben Samuel] picked up the skull
and began to turn it over in his hands.

'What are you looking for, John,' asked old Zach Laf-
foon.

'Bob Ford's bullet hole,' replied the bandit's half
brother; 'and here it is.'

There it was, a little more than an inch behind the left
ear and as large as a quarter."

So the hole in the back of the head was large, totally in keeping with a small bullet hole caused when the bullet entered
above the left eye and exited out in a larger hole behind the
left ear, both wounds made when the bullet entered the skull
in the front and exited in the back.

But in Homer Croy's book, he quotes the testimony of Bob
Ford himself, given during the inquest hearing after the shooting: (page 194)

"I was about eight feet from him when he [Jesse]
heard my pistol cock.

He turned his head like lightning. I fired, the ball

entering over the left eye and coming out behind the right ear."

Notice that Bob Ford stated he had shot him in the face, just what he would have had to say if Dalton had told him how he had shot Charlie Bigelow.

This testimony of Ford would be consistent with the claim of J. Frank Dalton who said that he shot Charlie Bigelow over the left eye, or right eye, according to Dalton's later report.

He would, of course, have had to tell Bob Ford how he had shot Charlie Bigelow because Bob was not present in the barn when Dalton shot Bigelow. Ford would have needed to know how the victim was shot so that his testimony would support the physical evidence when he was questioned by the various governmental bodies investigating the shooting.

There are some who have claimed that the injury over the left eye so visible in the photographs of the victim on the coroner's table was caused by the victim's head striking the wall after the shot to his head.

But this theory is refuted by the testimony of Charley Ford at the Coroner's Inquest. He testified:

"Q: Did he fall backward [after he was shot?]
A: He fell back toward me." DAILY GAZETTE, FRONT PAGE

Bob Ford's testimony was far more compelling. He was asked:

"Q: Did he fall off the chair on the floor?
A: Yes, he fell backward.

Q: You say he fell backwards?
A: Yes, he fell in the middle of the floor.
Q: Did he fall hard and strike his head?
A: No, sir; he came down tolerably easy.
                        DAILY GAZETTE, p. 4

So neither of the Ford Brothers claimed that the wound over the left eye was caused by the victim falling towards the wall before he fell to the floor.

This testimony is not conclusive, but it does seem to imply that these two "witnesses" did not see the body pitch forward and hit the wall before he "fell back toward" Charley. He repeated this observation a little later in the questioning:

"Q: When James fell, did he fall on his back or on his face?
A: On his back on the floor.
Q: Did you see any wound on his forehead?
A: I saw the blood shooting out." DAILY GA-ZETTE, front page

The story concocted by the real Jesse James worked. Even 118 years later, the people of America believe that Jesse James was shot by that "dirty little coward."

But Jesse knew differently!

chapter eight
JESSE'S PHONY STORY

There are at least three apparent problems with the official story of the shooting that an observant public should have recognized when they heard it for the first time:

1.   The story claimed that Jesse had taken his gun belt off in his own house.

It must be presumed that he had told Bob Ford to repeat this story that he had made up as a way of informing his friends and gang members, but not the public, that he was not dead, because they would have known that Jesse would have never taken his gun belt off during the day. He lived with his gun nearby at all times by necessity. It was certainly essential that he have one with him all of his waking hours, because it is known that people were anxious to shoot him, either for the reward money posted, or for the reputation that they were "the man who shot Jesse James."

Dalton claimed that he had killed Charlie Bigelow so that the world would believe that Jesse James was dead so that he could continue living his life under other aliases. He wanted to live his life without the fear of being shot. So he was certainly aware of the risks of living under the name of Jesse James. Yet the official story had him taking off his gun-belt. His friends must have laughed when they heard this part of the story. And they would have known from this supposed detail that Jesse had not died as the story claimed.

2.   The story claimed that he had been shot in the back of the head, yet the evidence showed that he had been

shot from the front.

This part of the story would have caused Jesse James to laugh as well as it circulated around the United States, because he knew that he had shot Charlie Bigelow in the face as he entered the barn. Yet history has recorded the story that he was shot in the back of the head.

3.   He claimed that he had stood on a chair to "dust off a picture" or to "straighten out a picture on the wall."

It is hard to believe that this part of the story stuck as well, as the public was being asked to believe that Jesse James, a "blood-thirsty murderer" would care enough about a little dust on a picture that he would take the time to dust it, or that the picture hanging on the wall was not straight and that he would have cared enough to straighten it.

The world believed this part of this entire story and Jesse must have been pleased that the media bought the entire phony package. The people believed it. He had succeeded in pulling it off.

In fact, J. Frank Dalton was quoted as saying: JJ AND THE LOST CAUSE, PAGE 22

"There are just a lot of people that will take anything they read as gospel facts.

No matter how corny, impossible, how big a lie it is, they just simply believe what they see written."

Once again, it can only be surmised that Jesse made up this entire story as a way of informing his friends and family around America that he was still alive, and, as could have been expected, stories began circulating shortly after his alleged death that he had survived the shooting.

On April 14, 1882, the Liberty, Missouri Tribune newspaper reported :

> "Certain parties still claim that Jesse James is not dead and intimate that the man killed and buried was not Jesse, but someone inveigled into Jesse's house and killed to get the reward."(p. 169 JESSE JAMES WAS HIS NAME by William A. Settle Jr.)

This reporter seems to be implying that it was the real Jesse James in the house in St. Joseph. I have examined this possibility in an earlier chapter and concluded that the man living in the house could not have been the real Jesse. This same author commented about another sighting:

> "Scarcely a year had passed, however, before a Clay County farmer was reported to have seen Jesse."

He reported that this observation came from an article in the St. Joseph Gazette on April 20, 1883, so the investigative reporter of the day certainly could have looked into the story and confirmed that Jesse was still alive. But the same author then makes this statement:

> "The identification [meaning the identification of the body by Zee James and Zarelda James Samuel] of the man who was shot in the Jameses' front room was positive enough to leave little doubt that the body buried in Mrs. Samuel's yard was Jesse James." (Page 169, JESSE JAMES WAS HIS NAME William A. Settle Jr.)

So it is clear that Mr. Settle didn't pursue such leads because he chose to believe that the man was dead.

And since the idea of a conspiracy in such a case as this seemed to be so far-fetched, no one believed it enough to see if it was real.

Jesse (meaning Dalton) himself feared that there were law men who knew he had staged the entire shooting and that his life was in danger even after the funeral. He is quoted as saying:

> ". . . after we pulled my fake funeral and hoax at St. Joseph, there were still some detectives not satisfied. They knew I wasn't dead and tried to prove I was not dead by fetching me in alive." JJ AND THE LOST CAUSE p. 159

So Jesse's plan had not totally succeeded. He still had reason to worry about some one recognizing him and doing him some harm after he had staged the fake shooting. But Jesse knew that those in the general public who had feared the fact that Jesse James was alive and stealing from or murdering the honest citizens of the day, certainly wanted him gone, and that they were apt to believe his story even when it was at odds with the facts, or was removed from simple logic.

So generally no one was listening. Everyone knew, because they wanted to believe, that Jesse had been killed in St. Joseph, Missouri on April 3, 1882. And that is the story generally accepted by the public today.

Only the real Jesse and those involved in assisting him in the murder of Charlie Bigelow knew that the story was not true: he was not dead!

chapter nine
THE MISSING
"MIDDLE FINGER"

There has been a question amongst the Jesse James researchers about the conclusion of some that the real Jesse James had lost the tip of his middle finger, (some say it was the entire finger above the knuckle,) on his left hand due to a gun accident when he was a young man, and that J. Frank Dalton did not exhibit any such injury.

One such comment was made in the book entitled THE MANY FACES OF JESSE JAMES: (page 75)

> "During his youth, Jesse James accidently shot off the tip of his middle left hand finger in a gun accident. His self-consciousness over his mangled finger is clearly visible in all authentic photos of him."

The author of this book then comments repeatedly about their observation that in the many pictures they have published of Jesse in their book, that he seems to be constantly clenching his left hand or hiding it in pockets or behind his back so that you cannot see the fingers on his left hand. This seems to be true after viewing the pictures they have assembled in their book.

Another author, Carl Briehan, states in his book that he is an authority on Jesse James and he is the one who pointed this out (according to Rudy Turilli:)

> "Jesse James had a missing middle finger."

Most James researchers say that he only had lost the top part of that middle finger, but here Mr. Briehan says it was the entire finger.

The Gazette newspaper of April 4, 1882 made this observation about the body of the man laying on he undertaker's table, after "Jesse James" was shot by Bob Ford:

"A further inspection of the body revealed . . . the absence of the tip of the middle finger of the left hand."

So reports like these appear to be the source of the "missing middle finger" or the "tip of the missing middle finger" story: it comes from the evidence on the body of the man shot as Jesse James (Source: the Rise and Fall of Jesse James, page 347) meaning if Dalton is correct, the body of Charlie Bigelow.

This is how Rudy Turilli discussed the charge on page 18 of his book entitled THE TRUTH ABOUT JESSE JAMES:

"I would like for Mr. Briehan to produce to the world any photograph showing Jesse James with his middle finger missing from his left hand."

So it appears that later critics of Dalton's story that he was Jesse James are claiming that if he was not missing this middle finger, he could not be the real Jesse James.

But there does appear to be a picture of a man missing what appears to be the top portion of that finger. And it is the picture of the man history has recorded as being the real Jesse James. If the observer looks carefully at the picture of the man on the autopsy table, it appears as if he is missing the top portion of his middle finger on his left hand.

But, of course, if Frank Dalton is correct, this picture is of the body of Charlie Bigelow and it was he who had a missing middle left finger and not Jesse James himself.

In other words, the story goes like this: friends of Jesse's claim that he lost a portion of a finger on his left hand when he was a young man. Then they spotted the missing tip of the middle finger on the man history has claimed was the real Jesse James. They then have concluded that this was the finger that was injured when he was a young man: the middle finger of his left hand.

So, according to this theory, the man shot in St. Joseph, Missouri, that day, must have been the real Jesse James.

But that poses a problem if Dalton is correct, because he is claiming that the man on the table is Charlie Bigelow, who was missing a portion of his middle finger on his left hand.

However, we need to examine the source of that story that Jesse had lost that portion of his finger, and if the story was told AFTER the autopsy was done on the body of the man identified as Jesse, then even that man might not have been the real Jesse since no historian that I can find wrote about the missing finger until the body was looked at.

I can find no credible report BEFORE the autopsy that Jesse had lost a portion of any finger prior to the autopsy. So, it could be that the story was made up to help identify the body of Charlie Bigelow as being that of the real Jesse James, the man with a "missing middle finger on his left hand."

However, when J. Frank Dalton died in 1951, the "post mortem identification of Jesse James" showed the following:

"Tip end sort of 'chewed' off of left index finger."

Numerous pictures were taken of Mr. Dalton between the years of 1948 and 1951, and one of these is taken from his left side and clearly show all of the fingers on his left hand. The tip of his left index finger appears to have been blackened under the nail as if he had hit it with a hammer. Now whether or not this is the "missing middle finger" that Mr. Briehan mentioned, is not known. It certainly could have changed from the "index finger" to the "middle finger" in the repeated telling of the story in the 66 years between Jesse and J. Frank Dalton, especially after the body of the alleged Jesse James showed that it had a portion of his left middle finger missing.

When J. Frank Dalton surfaced in 1948, the Lawton Oklahoma newspaper (page 8) made this observation about this injured finger when it was talking about the many injuries and wounds that Dalton had incurred:

"One in particular, which is known to the world, is a damaged left forefinger. It was injured when he was small when accidentally his older brother, Frank, caused an object to drop on it. The nail all these years has grown crooked."

So here we have another version of an injured finger on the left hand, but this time it is on the index finger rather than the "middle finger."

There is even another report of how Jesse injured his left index finger. This one comes from the book entitled JESSE JAMES -- THE OUTLAW by Henry J. Walker (page 83). He wrote:

". . . the end of that finger had been bitten off by a young fellow in a fight over a girl, at a box supper in 1862, near Mountain Grove, Missouri."

It certainly could be possible that the statements about the "missing middle left finger" are made about the missing left finger shown in the pictures of the alleged Jesse James lying on the mortician's table. Once again, if the reader looks carefully, it appears as if that man's hand is missing the top portion of the finger on his left hand.

But it is nearly impossible for anyone to know. However, there is still another possibility that must be examined.

One individual claims that the injury was only to the "left index finger." That story by John Pierce is reported in Rudy Turilli's book on pages 20-21 and is as follows:

"One identifying characteristic of the said Jesse James, among others, was that his index finger on his left hand had, early in life, been injured by a pistol shot in such a manner that the said finger was deformed at the tip, and was immediately noticeable."

Notice that Mr. Pierce reported that this injury was "early in his life," so it could have been the one that Mr. Briehan reported on, except that the details about what caused the injury have changed with time.

But the question must be asked: Is it possible that these two injuries are the same one? And that the details have changed with the passing of the years? And that J. Frank Dalton exhibits the correct injury to the injured left hand of the real Jesse James? And that the real Charlie Bigelow did not?

chapter ten
THE MONEY POWER

"Every loan [by a central bank] seats a Nation or upsets a Throne." attributed to Lord Byron

It might assist the reader at this point to break from the narrative on the life of Jesse James to explain a little about money and why people wish to possess huge quantities of it. Because it is clear that Jesse understood why it was important to accumulate money and how it could be made to work for the individual possessing it.

First let me explain that Jesse was a member of the banking fraternity. He had created a bank in 1870 in Deer Lodge, Montana and later a branch of the bank in Butte, Montana. His banking establishment was called the Donnell, Clark and Larabie Bank. So he had a personal interest in how bankers operated.

The word MONEY is defined as "a medium of exchange and measure of value."

That means that Jesse used money as a "measure of value" when he bought land or businesses. He set the value of the item purchased by a specified amount of money and then paid for it with that medium.

The traditional thinking has it that the way to wealth is to hire employees to make it for you. Produce a product or a service and sell it to the public, and if you sell enough of it, you will become wealthy.

But there is another way to wealth: use money!

Those who own money, the "money possessors," soon discovered that money had an advantage over employees. Both could be used to make money. But employees hired by the businessman want vacations, sick leave, holidays, etc. And they only work 8 hours a day and 40 hours a week, and then only on weekdays. Also, employees can cost the employer money when they don't produce.

But money needs no such fringe benefits. It works 365 days a year, 24 hours a day, meaning it works on holidays, receives no paid vacation and doesn't want sick leave.

So money accumulation, instead of employee production, became the goal of the greedy.

But those who accumulate money live in a constant fear that the money they save today won't be worth that amount tomorrow. They certainly hoped that it would keep the same value it possessed when it was saved, so that it would have the same purchasing power it had when it was set aside.

There is a word that defines the loss of value in money. It is called INFLATION. That word is defined as:

> INFLATION: A sudden increase in the quantity of money relative to the amount of exchange business.

Inflation always produces a rise in the price level. This makes any quantity of money decrease in value.

INFLATION is an economic law! That means that no matter who increases the money supply, there will ALWAYS be a price increase. An ECONOMIC LAW means that no matter who increases the quantity of money, or where on earth they do it, there will ALWAYS be a price rise.

Money can also increase in its value. This is defined as a DEFLATION:

DEFLATION: a sudden decrease in the quantity of money relative to the amount of exchange business.

Deflation always produces a lowering in the price level. This makes any quantity of money increase in value.

So, sudden increases or decreases in the quantity of money could cause price swings that could destroy the value of the money that Jesse and the others had accumulated.

The "money possessors" quickly learned that the only way they could prevent price inflations and deflations was to get control of the money supply themselves, to wrest it from the private banks in the United States. So it became apparent that the wealthy had to get control of the money machine, the ability to control the money supply itself.

In America, prior to the American Revolution of 1776, many local banks issued their own money based upon the amount of gold or silver they had deposited in the bank. The gold owner would bring the gold into the bank and be issued a "RECEIPT" for that gold, meaning that the bank would issue "gold receipts" (a piece of paper certifying the gold was on deposit) for the gold brought into the bank for safe keeping.

These "gold receipts" were marked "REDEEMABLE IN GOLD PAYABLE TO THE BEARER" which meant that the holder of the receipt could instantly demand that the bank return his or her gold by redeeming the receipt. In other words, the receipt owner would trade the paper for the gold on deposit in the bank. This system was called THE GOLD STANDARD.

The bankers soon perceived that there was a problem with "gold receipts:" the owners could always redeem them for their gold.

And the reason is clear: bankers had the ability to increase the money supply by issuing more "gold receipts" than there was gold on deposit, thereby decreasing the value of the "gold receipts" that they had already issued.

But the bankers soon realized that there was a "downside" to GOLD RECEIPT INFLATION: a "run" on a bank. This occurs when all of the depositors show up on the same day to redeem their gold receipts for their gold. The cause of the problem lies in the fact that the banker had issued too many gold receipts and there wasn't enough gold to honor all of the requests for it.

"Bank Runs" were the price the bankers had to pay for the crime of issuing too many gold receipts over and above the gold they had issued gold receipts for. So they devised a plan to issue only enough excess gold receipts to not alarm the other receipt holders that their gold was losing its value. The object was to increase the amount of receipts but not enough to cause a "bank run."

Because whenever the inflation became too severe, the people would redeem their receipts as a way to hedge against the lessening value. And generally the bankers who had fooled the people got caught in their scheme, and they would have to flee with their lives.

This of course did not lead to lengthy business tenures. Being an inflating banker usually had a short term life expectancy.

But the power to increase or decrease the money supply had

been placed into the hands of the federal government in the Constitution of the united States of America. Article 1, Section 8 of that document reads:

"The Congress shall have the power . . . to coin money, [and] regulate the value thereof . . . ."

So the bankers determined that they would not get caught if they could enlist the government as an ally.

They reasoned that if they could get the government to regulate the refunding of gold when the gold receipts were turned in, they could get government to make it a crime to own gold so that the bankers would not have to redeem their money when asked to do so.

And once they secured the assistance of the federal government to make it illegal to own gold, they could then increase and then decrease the quantity of money just as often as they wanted and make profits either way the price level went.

So the bankers had to get control of the banking system in each nation and then get that nation off of the gold standard so that they could more properly control the quantity of money.

They quickly determined that if they could buy politicians with their money, they could get these politicians to pass laws making it a crime to own gold and that everyone had to accept the new receipts issued by the banks that were not redeemable in gold.

And they coined two new words: LEGAL TENDER, to cover their crime. The government required the gold owner to accept a piece of paper that was not redeemable in his gold because the politicians had passed a law making it illegal to own gold. Then each seller of goods had to accept the inflated money because the government had made it LEGAL TENDER, meaning they had to accept the irredeemable paper money when the owner used them to pay off a debt. And the person owed the debt had to accept the new money.

The transition from a "GOLD STANDARD" to a "PAPER STANDARD" (a system where the money was not backed by gold but by the number of the paper receipts issued) was the way the local banks got control of the money supply.

Perhaps this can best be illustrated by these phrases printed on the face of the American money and how these words changed over the years:

The original money issued in America had this phrase printed on its face:

> "This is to certify that there is on deposit at the U.S. Treasury 'X' dollars in gold payable to the bearer on demand."

Notice that this money guaranteed that there was enough gold on hand to redeem ALL gold receipts.

That phrase was changed in 1928 to:

> "Redeemable in gold on demand at the U.S. Treasury or in lawful money at any Federal Reserve bank."

(The critic of the system used to ask this question after reading this statement: if the possessor could redeem the paper money and get "lawful money" for it, did that mean that the possessor's money was "unlawful" before he turned it in to receive "lawful money" in exchange for it? And the answer had to be: it would have had to have been "UNLAWFUL MONEY.") (Even today, this is still a legitimate question!)

Here the government allowed the "money possessors" in the banking system to redeem the "gold receipts" with either gold or "lawful money," at their discretion.

And these words changed again in 1934:

> "this note is legal tender for all debts, public and private and is redeemed in lawful money at the treasury or at any federal reserve bank."

Here the ability to obtain gold in exchange for the paper when turned in has been totally removed. Now the holder could only get "lawful money" for his paper.

And the phrase changed again in 1963 to what is on the American money today:

> "this note is legal tender for all debts, public and private."

Now the money possessor cannot even get "lawful money" for his "unlawful money!"

Today's holder of paper money can see this phrase on the upper left hand corner of the front side.

So there is no redemption of the receipt for gold any longer. This right of the people has simply vanished.

This means that the citizens of a nation could not create their own money any longer, they could not circulate anything but these paper certificates as money, and that they couldn't own gold as a store of value against the phony paper receipts. They could only circulate the paper money issued by the bankers.

The bankers love the "PAPER STANDARD" (once again, a standard where money is not backed by a precious metal, but is backed by the word of the government, and the quantity of money is controlled by the bankers.) They can issue as much of it as they wish, and they have gotten the government to make it legal to pay debts with it.

But the key to the "PAPER STANDARD" is the ability of the bankers to loan money to the government, at interest.

Just as a private individual borrows money from a bank when he or she needs it for the purchase of some large dollar item, the government has a bank that it borrows from when it needs to pay its bills. It is called A CENTRAL BANK.

Governments frequently operate on a "deficit," meaning they spend more money than they take in. They need to borrow from the bankers to pay their bills and the bankers have created a "central bank" to loan the government the needed money.

The advantage to this banking system is that the bankers possess a monopoly on loaning money to the government (this writer will concede that the government does borrow money from the private sector, meaning individuals, but this is generally only a small percentage of the population and for a small percentage of the entire debt.) The government does not borrow from the private sector (in the main,) it borrows from the central bank, owned by the bankers.

And the purpose of making the people think that they are the ones who loan the money to the government, is to perpetuate the myth that the "people owe this debt to the people." The truth is that this statement is not true: it is in the main borrowed from the "CENTRAL BANK."

When the nation borrows money to pay their deficits, the central bankers loan the nation the money it needs to pay their bills. But the reason the bankers love this process is the ability of the "CENTRAL BANK" to loan money to the government AT INTEREST, so that the government can buy what it cannot afford.

Just as the state bank charges interest for the privilege of borrowing money, so does the central bank: they charge the nation interest on the money that they loan the government. The "CENTRAL BANK" does not have to actually have the money on deposit, they have been given the "right" to print the money and loan it to the government when they do not possess enough money on deposit. That means they have the ability to print paper money out of nothing.

This is interesting because anyone who owns a printing press, ink and paper can increase the quantity of money by simply printing it. However, when an individual prints money out of nothing and is discovered by the F.B.I., they are arrested and charged with "counterfeiting." Counterfeiting is a crime against the legal money holders, because it increases the money supply, thereby dropping the value of the good money in circulation. This is why it is a punishable crime: it destroys a "property right," the right of the money holders to a reasonably constant value of their personal property: their money.

But the bankers have the identical ability: they can print up money out of nothing. But in their case, the government has made it "LEGAL TENDER" and not a crime of "counter-

124

feiting." In other words, the bankers can "counterfeit" and it is not called "counterfeiting." The government allows them to make their money LEGAL TENDER: the people have to accept it in exchange for their goods or services.

Once this process is understood, American history will start to make enormous sense, because American history has been the battle of the "money possessors" to get control of a nation's money supply by creating a "central bank," granted the exclusive right to print paper money and then the power to loan it to the government at interest.

And Jesse James was right in the middle of this battle. Jesse and his banking friends finally succeeded with the passage of The Federal Reserve Bill in 1913, because this bill created the essential ingredient to making the scheme work: THE FEDERAL RESERVE BANK, this nation's privately owned central bank.

There are now a growing number of historians, the present writer being one of the first, that see a continuous thread through the first 137 years of this nation.

We have discovered that America's history from 1776 through the passage of the Federal Reserve Bill in 1913 has a common thread through all of that period: the desire of the bankers to create a privately owned banking system, a "CENTRAL BANK," that would have the power to create money out of nothing, loan it to the government and collect the interest on the debt the government had created.

And this started in the years around the American Revolution of 1776.

chapter eleven
THE MONEY POWER
CONQUERS AMERICA

Those of us who are only vaguely familiar with American history might remember that there was a debate between Alexander Hamilton and Thomas Jefferson, two of America's founding fathers, about the need to create "a central bank" with the powers desired by the bankers. Hamilton was in favor of creating such a " central bank," and Jefferson was in opposition.

The lines were drawn when Hamilton stated his position:

> "No society could succeed which did not unite the interest and credit of rich individuals with those of the state. A national debt, if it is not excessive, will be to us a national blessing." (Quoted in THE CREATURE FROM JEKYLL ISLAND by Ed Griffin, page 329)

Honest historians have recorded the statements by Jefferson that clearly show his opposition to the view of Hamilton and the bankers. He is quoted as saying:

> "The principle of spending money to be paid by posterity, [meaning future generations] under the name of funding, [meaning paying for tomorrow's governmental needs by borrowing from the banks at interest today] is but swindling futurity on a large scale."

> "Banking establishments are more dangerous to the liberties of a nation than standing armies."

Others of Jefferson's warnings were clear and to the point:

"If the American people ever allow private banks to control the issue of currency, first by inflation, then by deflation, the banks and corporations that will grow up around them will deprive the people of all property until their children will wake up homeless on the continent their fathers conquered." (Quoted on page 247. H.S. Kennan, The Federal Reserve)

Jefferson certainly knew that the banks then in existence were PRIVATE BANKS, but they were chartered by the states. I believe that he was referring to A PRIVATELY OWNED CENTRAL BANK created by the federal government.

So Thomas Jefferson clearly understood the principles in the debate. He argued against the creation of a national bank; Alexander Hamilton argued in favor.

Unfortunately for the American people, Hamilton won the debate, and the government created the first Bank of the United States in 1791. This bank was privately owned, had the power to print government money, loan it back to the government, and collect the interest, just like today's Private Reserve (this author is on a one man crusade to ask the American people to call "the Federal Reserve" what it truly is: a Private banking Reserve operating under the cover of being "Federal." It isn't.)

And the reader is encouraged to prove it for themselves by finding a city phone directory in a city where there is a branch of the Private Reserve, and attempt to locate their phone number in the Blue Pages, meaning the pages that list all of the governmental agencies. The number will not be found there.

However, when you look for their listing in the white pages

containing the names of the private businesses, you will find them listed under the "F's" like other businesses with the first name FEDERAL in their names. So please join me in calling it what it is: The Private Reserve!)

The debate was on, and those in favor won the first round.

As a compromise to those in opposition, the supporters of this nation's first central bank only wrote the charter for 20 years, rather than creating it for perpetuity. So the charter that the government granted this privately owned bank was to run from 1791 to 1811 when it was scheduled to expire.

There were calls for the federal government to renew the charter, but in 1811, it was not renewed by President James Monroe, and this nation's first privately owned national bank went out of business.

But the European bankers were not finished.

They had not succeeded in their attempt to create a permanent national bank in America. So they met again.

And the result was the War of 1812 between England and the United States.

The first bank charter expired in 1811, and there was a war involving the United States and the English government in 1812. (Remember that the American Revolution was also fought between England and the United States.)

The bankers had not succeeded in their goal, so they planned another war to create similar conditions to those in the first war between England and the United States, called the American Revolutionary War.

Now this quote by Thomas Jefferson will make sense:

"It is incumbent on every generation to pay its own debts as it goes -- a principle which if acted on, would save one half of the wars of the world."

Jefferson understood the connection between debt and war: bankers love wars because they enable "central banks" to make enormous profits on the loaning of their newly created money to the government, at interest!

Bankers make enormous profits from wars because governments need to borrow huge sums of money to pay for it. And they turn to the nation's bank, the "CENTRAL BANK," to borrow it. And in fact, more profits can be made if the central banks make loans to both sides in a war.

And anyone familiar with European history knows that Europe has been plagued for centuries with wars between the central bank of one nation and the central bank of another.

George Washington, this nation's first President, understood this as well. He warned America in the last speech he gave as President of the United States (called his Farewell Address):

"It is our true policy to steer clear of permanent alliances with any portion of the foreign world . . . .

Why, by interweaving our destiny with that of any part of Europe, entangle our peace and prosperity in the toils of European ambition, [and] rivalship . . .?"

But by 1811, the American people had forgotten the advice of their President, and allowed the English bankers to start the War of 1812.

That war lasted for about three years. Those who favored the war had forced the American government to find a way to pay for it, and those who favored the war also favored the creation of a second Bank of the United States, and one was created in 1816. This bank also had a 20 year charter, meaning that this charter would come up for renewal in 1836.

The President in 1832 was Andrew Jackson, a great American hero. He resisted the renewal of the charter of the second bank, and was quoted as saying that he held:

". . . the belief that some of the powers and privileges possessed by the existing bank [the second bank] are unauthorized by the Constitution, subversive of the rights of the States, and dangerous to the liberties of the people . . . ."

President Jackson made his dissatisfaction about the bank well known to the American people. He was quoted as saying:

"I was one of those who do not believe that a national bank is a national blessing, but rather a curse to a republic inasmuch as it is calculated to raise around the administration a money aristocracy dangerous to the liberties of the country." the Age of Jackson, Arthur M. Schlesinger, page 18

Because of his strong dislike of the bank, Jackson made the renewal of the charter the sole issue of the 1832 Presidential election. He ran for the Presidency on a simple platform:

"Bank and no Jackson, or Jackson and no bank."

One later American President, **Franklin Roosevelt** wrote a letter in about 1933 in which he admitted that the battle of

Jackson's time had a winner:

> "The real truth of the matter is, as you and I know, that a financial element . . . has owned the government since the days of Andrew Jackson." Arthur M. Schlesinger, THE COMING OF THE NEW DEAL)

And Jackson won the election (what do you think his chances would be today if he ran on a similar platform: "Private Reserve Bank and no Jackson, or Jackson and no Private Reserve Bank?" First of all, it would be my opinion that the American people would generally not understand the issue, because they have not been taught how central banks function, and, secondly, I believe that the bankers would make certain that they didn't understand the issue and because of that, Jackson would lose!)

But, fortunately for America, the voters of 1832 did understand and Jackson won the election by the largest margin ever afforded an American president up to that point. And the bankers showed their displeasure at that vote by arranging for an assassination attempt on his life: President Jackson was the victim of the first assassination attempt ever made on any American president.

The day was January 30, 1835, and Richard Lawrence, the man who made the attempt on Jackson's life, was quoted as saying:

> "I've been in touch with the powers in Europe, [could this mean that Lawrence had been in touch with the "central bankers" of Europe? I think so] which have promised to intervene if any attempt was made to punish me."

The assassination attempt failed and Jackson was not injured.

So the charter for America's second central bank lapsed in 1836, twenty years after it had been created in 1816.

But the European bankers had not finished with America. They had not obtained their Private Reserve.

So they planned another war.

This one was called the Civil War.

Jesse James in his youth. This if the photograph
commonly used as the official one.

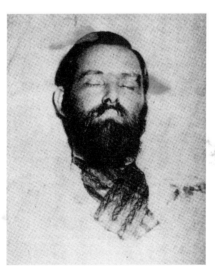

Jesse James in 1882 after he was shot. Many do not see
the resemblance between this and the picture above.

**The official picture of Jesse James, believed to be
J. Frank Dalton, and Sen. William Andrews Clark**

**J. Frank Dalton at 101 years of age,
believed to be the real Jesse James.**

**Sen. William Andrews Clark, believed to be the real
Jesse James under an alias.**

**J. Frank Dalton at 101 years of age, believed to be
the real Jesse James under another alias.**

John Wilkes Booth, the Lincoln assassin, reportedly shot in 1865. Dalton claimed he poisoned him in 1903.

The mummy of John Wilkes Booth, as photographed by Life Magazine in 1930.

Zarelda James, the mother of Jesse James. Notice that part of her right arm is missing.

Brothers Jesse and Frank James, giving hand signs that they are Masons or Knights of the Golden Circle.

Zarelda James standing by the tombstone of Jesse James, on her farm in Kearney, Missouri.

The house where J. Frank Dalton claimed he shot Charlie Bigelow, a fake Jesse James.

**Allen Pinkerton, giving the secret sign indicating
he was a member of the Masons.**

**"Bloody Bill" Anderson, of the Quantrill Raiders, giv-
ing the secret sign he was a member of the K.G.C.**

Civil War photographer Matthew Brady's picture of the OSLIABA, a Russian ship in northern waters.

The Baltimore, Maryland Proclamation welcoming the Russian Fleet to the waters of the United States.

chapter twelve
THE CIVIL WAR, Part 1

But the bankers who needed another war in America to convince the government to create a PERMANENT Central Bank, faced a problem: who could they get to attack the United States in a war?

The problem was this: the bankers realized that England and France, or any other European country, or combination of countries, were 3,000 miles away from America, across an ocean, and that made supplying their troops in the United States, if they sent them, a real problem. And the reason was becoming clearer: America was a growing sea power, so that any European nation which attacked America would face not only a land war, but a naval war as well. The European nations would risk their naval power in an attempt to supply their land forces in a war against the United States.

So they had to look elsewhere for a warring enemy, and the first place they looked was on the North American continent itself.

Nearby neighbors Canada and Mexico had no ocean to cross in a war against the United States, but they were too small: they simply did not have the necessary economic strength to wage a war against the more powerful United States.

So the decision was reached in Europe to have America attack itself: they would divide the United States into two regions, a North and a South, and have them wage the war.

But they needed an issue other than the one Jackson ran his

1832 campaign on: the central bank. So in 1837, the bankers created a secret organization known as the Knights of the Golden Circle and sent their agents into the United States where they were instructed to use the issue of slavery as the issue to divide the United States into a North and a South.

J. Frank Dalton was aware of this secret society created in Europe. He wrote that:

> "Agents at work in Europe recruited German, Austrian, French and Italian tradesmen, and ex-soldiers who had served well in their own countries and were persuaded to move to America. The Knights of the Golden Circle financed them, but first they had to take an oath of utter secrecy." (JESSE JAMES AND THE LOST CAUSE, page 33)

Dalton explained how this organization provided for their members:

> "The Knights of the Golden Circle financed them, but first they had to take a blood oath of utter secrecy. After a probation period, they were then moved . . . into good jobs . . . ."(page 33 of JESSE JAMES AND THE LOST CAUSE)

Some of their members were moved into politics. Dalton reported:

> "Because our men were in the offices of public officials, . . . Congressmen, senators . . . ." JESSE JAMES AND THE LOST CAUSE page 35

And again on page 45 of JESSE JAMES AND THE LOST CAUSE:

"The Knights of the Golden Circle set up direct con-
nections with not only the European nations, but nations in South [America,] Cental America and the Or-
ient, not to forget we had any number of 'friends' operating in Canada and England too."

And their strategy worked: the Civil War between the North
and the South started in 1861, and America's history books
have reported that the war was fought over the issue of SLA-
VERY. But that was not the main issue: it was the desire of
the European bankers to create a "central bank" in America
after both the American Revolution and the War of 1812 had
failed to deliver the goal of the bankers. Of course, there had
to be an issue to get brother to fight brother, and that issue
was Slavery. But, in truth, those planning the war knew what
their goal was: America needed another central bank! And
this time, it had to be a PERMANENT central bank.

Abraham Lincoln was elected the President of the United
States in 1860, and inaugurated in 1861. After the war started,
he was approached by the European bankers who suggested
that he borrow the money the North needed to fund the war,
at 18 to 36% interest a year.(Appleton Cyclopedia, 1861, page
296) And they were pleased to be able to be the North's bankers and provide the necessary money.

Lincoln turned their offer down and printed up $450 million
in a new money, called "the Greenback," that was not borrowed from anyone, to pay for the costs of the war. He was
certainly aware of the dangers the bankers posed to the nation.
He tried to warn the American people:

"The money power preys upon the nation in times of
peace and conspires against it in times of adversity. I
see in the near future a crisis [that] causes me to trem-

143

ble for the safety of my country.

The money power will endeavor to prolong its reign
by working upon the prejudices of the people, and the
wealth is aggregated in a few hands, and the republic
is destroyed."

Congress suspended the gold standard in December of 1861,
and borrowed over $2 billion in long term bonds. (THE
GOLD RING, page 46) This had to be an effort to appease the
American bankers who were working with the European
bankers, because Lincoln decided to print his own money.

So the bankers decided that Lincoln had to be removed. He
had dared to cross the "money possessors."

More recently, President John Kennedy (1961-1963) also
printed money that was not borrowed from the bankers. He
called his money U S Bank Notes, the same name that Lincoln had used when he created his "greenback." The money
that both of these men issued was just issued, with no re-
sulting interest payments to the bankers.

President Lincoln attended a play on April 15, 1865, and never came back!

President Kennedy was sent to Dallas, Texas on November
22, 1963 and never came back!

Upon the death of John Kennedy, Lyndon Johnson, his Vice
President, assumed the Presidency. One of his first official
acts was to call in this new money. In fact, he did this just
days after he assumed the office, almost as if he knew that
this was something he HAD to do.)

But even with the death of Abraham Lincoln, the bankers had not achieved their goal: there was no permanent central bank in place in America.

And Lincoln's successor in office, Vice President **Andrew Johnson**, didn't offer them any resolution either. He gave a speech in which he chose to identify the same enemy that Lincoln had identified. **Johnson** said:

> "The tendency of the legislation of this country is to build up monopolies, . . . to build up the money power . . . to concentrate power in the hands of a few. The tendency is against the great mass of the people." (REVOLUTION AFTER LINCOLN, by Claude G. Bowers, page 30)

So **Johnson** had clearly aligned himself with Abraham Lincoln: he knew who had planned the Civil War. So the bankers attempted to remove him from office by the Constitutional process called Impeachment: they were successful in that he was impeached, but they were unsuccessful in that they were unable to acquire the necessary votes to remove him from office. They came within one vote of their goal.

It is quite likely that after this vote, the overall plans of the bankers were changed.

The result of all of this planning was clear: they had failed each time. They had removed Abraham Lincoln, but could not remove **Andrew Johnson**. They had created at least two central banks, but not a permanent one.

Each time they had fought a war against the people of the United States, (the American Revolution of 1776, the War of 1812, and now the Civil War,) they had not secured the one thing they so desperately wanted: a permanent "central bank."

So they had to change their strategy.

And change it they did.

But only after they had removed Abraham Lincoln as a lesson to future Presidents not to cross the "central bankers," and after the Civil War had ended in 1865.

chapter thirteen
THE CIVIL WAR, part 2

Jesse James and his brother Frank both played a minor role in the American Civil War (1861-1865) but Jesse played a far more significant role in the period after it. And it becomes important to study the Civil War far more closely than most historians have in the past.

History has recorded the role in this war of a group of Southern sympathizers known as **Quantrill**'s Raiders led by **William Clarke Quantrill**. They were active in Kansas and Missouri during the Civil War and it has been written that both Frank and Jesse James had joined his group. A book entitled FRANK AND JESSE JAMES by Ted P. Yeatman (page 35) quoted Frank in 1901 as saying that he "joined **Quantrill** in May, 1863." (This date is open to dispute. I prefer to believe my research which has indicated that the date was 1862. This will be discussed a little later.)

But in Jesse's case, it has been reported that he had joined a band led by "Bloody Bill" Anderson, a "lieutenant" of Quantrill's who had accepted Jesse after he had been turned down by **Quantrill** himself because of his youth (Jesse was only 14 or 15 in 1862.) Anderson apparently had no qualms about accepting the youthful Jesse in his branch of the **Quantrill**'s Raiders.

But Jesse's major role in the period around the Civil War occurred after it had ended.

Sometime during the war itself or shortly thereafter, Jesse joined a 14,000 member organization known as The Knights

147

of the Golden Circle. They were formed in 1837, 24 years before the Civil War started. As discussed previously, their original backing came from a group of English and European bankers who had wanted to create a war in America so that the Union government of President Abraham Lincoln would have to borrow money to pay for the costs of the war from a central bank that they would gladly create and own.

For reasons already discussed, these bankers made the devision to divide the United States into a North and a South and to have the Northern states in America fight the war against their fellow Americans from the South. The organization known as the Knights of the Golden Circle was organized to create a mood of secession from the United States government amongst the Southern States. They used the issue of slavery to divide the 11 Southern states from the remaining 23 states in the Union.

Lincoln sensed that the two nations of England and France were conspiring against the United States. He realized that the South was primarily agrarian (meaning agriculturally based) and that it would need to import the strategic war-making technology it needed to wage the war. Two of the principal suppliers of these items would be the nations of England and France, both having "central banks" owned by the private bankers in their respective nations.

England and France were naval powers at the time and both were interested in supporting the South through the sale of this technology. (In a later chapter of this book, we will examine how J.P. Morgan, America's "banker," would make two visits to London, England, and Paris, France, before he created the "Panic of 1907." The reason he visited these two cities is because both of these nations had a privately owned "central bank," owned by the international bankers. And he had to get their permission to create the bank run associated with the banking event planned for 1907. So Lincoln knew that both of these nations were involved in America's Civil War because he had clearly stated that he feared the "money power.")

Lincoln decided to use the United States Navy to form a blockade of the Southern states in an attempt to cut off the supplies that they needed to sustain their war-making efforts.

Blockade running became a very profitable endeavor for those willing to run the risk. Judah Benjamin, the Secretary of State for the Confederacy, commented:

> "But we must already, before the first half-year of the blockade is over, offer blockade-runners a profit of fifty percent over the cost of the articles specially named, with reimbursement of all charges for 'freight, drayage, package, and cost of loading at the port of departure.'
>
> For freight, you will be allowed twice the current rates of freight from the port of loading . . . ." (Page 246 of JUDAH P. BENJAMIN by Butler)

So the South was encouraging its citizens to engage in blockade running. They were instructing their people that money could be made in running Lincoln's blockade.

President Lincoln's blockade obviously angered the bankers in the two nations. So they countered his blockade with plans of their own.

The bankers decided to support the South by arranging for France to build freight carrying ships that would be so heavily armed that they would be able to break through Lincoln's blockade.

Lincoln quickly realized that he needed a naval ally.

Almost all of the European nations were controlled by some sort of central bank owned by a consortium of the international bankers. There was only one nation in all of Europe that had no such central bank and that was the nation of Russia.

So in 1863, Lincoln and Alexander II, the Czar of Russia, negotiated a pact wherein the Czar agreed to send his navy, then the world's largest, into the ports of New York City and San Francisco, as a means of not so subtly notifying the European nations, primarily England and France, that the Russians were aligning themselves with Lincoln's government. The Czar then issued orders to his admirals that they were to take orders from no one but Abraham Lincoln himself, and that if they were fired upon by any European nation, they were authorized to return fire, and by that act, Russia would then be at war with that nation.

The most famous photographer of the Civil War was Matthew Brady, and I have found three of his photographs of the Osliaba, one of these Russian ships in a northern port during 1863. So photographic evidence does exist of the Russian ships in the ports of the North. I have also found a drawing of a Russian ship in the port of New York in a book written by a Russian writer. Apparently the Russians are told more about the role of Russia in America's Civil War than are the Americans, because Civil War historians generally fail to mention the visit of the Russian navy in the ports of the North.

Another item of interest to confirm this part of the Civil War story is a proclamation issued by the City of Baltimore, Maryland on October 5, 1863. This document reads, in part:

"Resolutions providing for inviting the Officers of the Russian frigates to visit the City of Baltimore . . . to accept its hospitalities as a Testimonial of the high respect of the authorities and Citizens of Baltimore for the Sovereign [meaning Czar Alexander II] and people of Russia, who, when other powers and people more strongly bound to us by the ties of interest or common descent have lent material and moral aid to the Rebels of the South, have honorably abstained from all attempts to assist the rebellion and have given our Government reliable assurances of their sympathy and good will."

The "other powers more strongly bound to us" must have been England and France, who were lending their support to the South during the Civil War. It appears as if the city fathers of Baltimore were referring to these two nations who they believed had more reason to support the North than did Russia.

After the Russian fleet docked in American waters, England and France then canceled the orders to build the blockade-running ships, and for all practical purposes, pulled out of the war. The South was on its own.

In 1867, after the war was over, President **Andrew Johnson**, who had become President upon the assassination of Abraham Lincoln, received a bill for $7.2 million from the Russian government for the "rental" of the Russian fleet. The President knew that there was but one Constitutional method by which he could take American tax dollars to pay the Russian government for any reason. He realized that the only legal method by which he could pay this bill was to purchase land from that government. And the reason is in the Constitution of the united States of America: there is no provision authorizing the giving of federal tax moneys to any foreign nation for any reason, except for the purchase of land.

Perhaps the best example of this ability occurred in 1803 when the American government purchased a huge portion of the United States from France in what as been called The Louisiana Purchase.

Decisions were made in the **Johnson** administration to have Secretary of State William Seward purchase Alaska from the Russian government as a legal method of paying for the use of the Russian fleet.

Historians have called this purchase "Seward's folly," after the Secretary who negotiated the purchase for the American government. But it was not a "folly" at all, because if Russia had not intervened on the side of the North, it is quite likely that the North would have lost the war, especially if England and France had been allowed to complete the blockade runing ships.

(It is quite conceivable that the South that was supported by the European bankers, was never intended to win the Civil War. The purpose of the bankers was to make the prosecution of the Civil War as time consuming as possible, thereby raising the costs of the War itself. The ultimate purpose was to increase the pressure on the government of President Lincoln to do either of two things:

1.   borrow money from the European bankers or
2.   create the central bank that they so desperately desired,

152

as a way of paying for the enormous costs of the war. If they could not persuade his administration to borrow the money, they had hoped they could persuade Congress to create a "central bank" that would be owned by them. They were not able to do either.)

The Knights of the Golden Circle planned the assassination of Abraham Lincoln, and it was carried out on the night of April 14, 1865. They were able to accomplish it through their association with **John Wilkes Booth**, a member of the organization, and at least eight other conspirators.

(I have a copy of a book in my personal library that was issued only four months after the Lincoln assassination. This book is entitled THE ASSASSINATION AND HISTORY OF THE CONSPIRACY, by Bert James Loewenberg, Consulting Editor. This book makes this startling conclusion about the Knights of the Golden Circle: (on page 34)

". . . this order originated the plot to assassinate Abraham Lincoln."

Yet few historians of today even acknowledge the existence of this secret society in their writings on the Civil War. And if they do at all, they do not mention their direct involvement in the assassination of the President.)

The plans were made by the Knights for four men to be assassinated that night:

Abraham Lincoln
President of the United States, (the North;)
Andrew Johnson
Lincoln's Vice President;

William Seward
>the Secretary of State; and

Ulysses S. Grant
>then the Commander in Chief of the United
>States Army, and later President of the United
>States

If all of these men had been assassinated that night, the most logical man to assume the Presidency would have been **Edwin M. Stanton**, the Secretary of War.

It is an unanswered question of history as to why Secretary **Stanton** refused the President's request to be his guest and attend the play that the President and his wife were attending the night he was shot in Ford's Theater. Secretary **Stanton** refused, stating that he was "too busy" with the responsibilities of his office as the reason.

So the President and his wife attended the play without Secretary **Stanton**.

Someone else was invited to attend the play with the Lincolns and that was General Ulysses Grant. In fact, local newspapers reported that he and his wife would be in attendance in the theater that night.

However, the Grants were seen fleeing the city in a carriage before the play, and it is possible that General Grant had somehow learned of the planned attempt on his life.

It is quite possible that it was Secretary **Stanton** who warned them about their being on the short list of people to be assassinated that night.

There is reason to believe that the bankers wanted General

Grant to be spared and to later become President of the United States. And that reason was summarized in this quotation from the book entitled THE GOLD RING (page 49):

"President Grant made a campaign promise in 1868 to repay the war debt in gold, which bought joy to the bankers who had footed the original bill for Lincoln's army.

'To protect the national honor, every dollar of the Government indebtedness should be paid in gold,' Grant announced in his March 4, 1869 inaugural address."

This inaugural pledge was a fulfillment of a law passed by Congress in February, 1862 called The Legal Tender Act, which:

"authorized the Treasury to issue paper greenback dollars to be recognized as legal tender on all domestic obligations except customs duties and INTEREST ON THE NATIONAL DEBT." (Emphasis by Epperson) (THE GOLD RING, page 60)

So the people of America had to accept the unbacked Greenback dollar, but the bankers could only be paid legally in money backed by gold.

And this quotation will show the reader how much the bankers loaned the North during the war:

"The U.S. national debt rose from $64 million to over $2.8 billion between June 30, 1860 and September 1, 1865." (THE GOLD RING, page 67)

So, as was stated by Thomas Jefferson in that quotation printed above, the bankers love debt, and they raised the national debt 43.75 times during the war. And they were paid back in gold for their loans. The people of America were not.

It is interesting to observe how these activities could change the views of some of the people in Lincoln's cabinet, according to THE GOLD RING: (page 61):

> "Salmon Chase, when he was Abraham Lincoln's Treasury secretary, the same political animal who had designed the greenback system, now denounced the unredeemable paper currency."

Mr. Chase was rewarded with his reversal by being named Chief Justice of the Supreme Court.

And banks were named after him. The Chase Manhattan Bank of New York, a Rockefeller family owned bank, is named after Salmon P. Chase.

So, General Grant was "too busy" to attend the play that night with the President, but the bankers were not "too busy" to collect gold for the money they loaned the government to finance a war that they had planned years in advance.

After the Lincolns had been seated in a 2nd floor box on the side of the stage, and during the play, **Booth** walked into the room and fired a small derringer pistol into the back of his head, mortally wounding the President. His body was carried across the street into a rooming house where he later died.

One of the men who appeared while Lincoln was dying in that room was Secretary of War **Stanton**, then not "too busy" to visit the dying man. Most historians have not questioned the fact that **Stanton** was "too busy" to attend the play with Lincoln, but within minutes after the assassination, was not "too busy" to certify that Lincoln had died.

After the shooting, **Stanton**, in his official capacity as Secretary of War, issued orders to Northern troops to block the exit ways out of Washington D.C. It was presumed by the Secretary that **Booth** would want to escape the city that night and **Stanton** moved to block his escape routes. There were eight roads leading out of the city that could have been traveled by **Booth** after he had shot the President, and **Booth** happened to travel out on the one, known as the road to the Navy Yard Bridge, that **Stanton** did NOT issue orders to block. This bridge led to the state of Maryland, meaning to the South.

This omission on his part has generally been disregarded by historians but it strongly implies that **Stanton** was in support of the assassination plans of **Booth** and assisted him by not blockading the very exit that both knew **Booth** would take.

To my knowledge, there was no investigation into how **Booth** had escaped the city, over a route not blockaded by the Secretary of War. Apparently the government authorities must have reasoned that it was just an "innocent error," one that neither had to be investigated, nor one that had to be punished.

Civil War historians have claimed that **Booth** was later shot and killed in a barn near Bowling Green, Virginia, after being found by Northern troops searching for him. This action ended the story on **Booth** and completed the case against him as the assassin of Lincoln.

However, evidence has now been located that shows that

Booth did not die in the barn after all, but that it was another man, a Southern Captain by the name of James William Boyd, who was shot. (Notice that this Captain had the same initials as **John Wilkes Booth**.) It is now known that prior to his being in the barn, Boyd had been found in a Northern prison with a badly wounded RIGHT leg. He had been offered his freedom if he would ride down the route that **Stanton** knew **Booth** would travel, but he did not know that **Stanton** had planned to shoot him and then claim that he was **Booth**, the assassin of Lincoln.

And this is exactly what happened.

So the man shot as **Booth** was not **Booth**, but a Southern Captain, pressed into service by Secretary of War **Edwin Stanton**.

Stanton later visited the site where the body of Boyd was being autopsied and officially certified that it was the body of **John Wilkes Booth**. However, there were at least four major discrepancies between Boyd and **Booth** which **Stanton** could have noted if he had honestly conducted a review of the facts:

1.   Boyd was in his 40's, and **Booth** was 26;

2.   Boyd had a wounded RIGHT leg, and **Booth** had broken his LEFT leg after he jumped to the stage in the theater after shooting Lincoln;

3.   Boyd had a mustache, as did **Booth**, but he (**Booth**) had shaved his off after the shooting during his visit to the home of Samuel Mudd, a doctor who treated him for his broken leg,

4.   Boyd had reddish-brown hair and **Booth** had coal

black hair.

Nevertheless, **Stanton** certified that the body of Boyd was that of **Booth**, and then had him buried behind the walls of a Northern prison so that no one could exhume it and state that it was not the body of **Booth**.

So the story on the assassination of Abraham Lincoln ended with the burial of the body of "**John Wilkes Booth**."

The diary kept by **John Wilkes Booth** prior to the assassination has now surfaced and is currently on display at Ford's Theater in Washington D.C. It is shown being held open by two panes of glass at the precise section where the visitor can see that 18 pages have been cut out.

These 18 pages were reportedly located in the attic of one of **Stanton**'s descendants and according to the book entitled THE LINCOLN CONSPIRACY by David Balsiger and Charles E. Sellier, Jr., these pages contained:

"The names of 70 prominent people directly and indirectly involved in **Booth**'s plan to kidnap Lincoln." (page 11)

"The plan to kidnap Lincoln" was the original plan of the **Booth** conspirators, but they had to modify these plans when their efforts to kidnap Lincoln failed. Their plans changed from kidnaping the President to assassinating the President.

These authors identified five of these men by publishing their photographs (on an unnumbered page after page 160) accompanied by this paragraph:

"Northern commodities speculators and financiers of

the Union war effort conspired to have Lincoln force-
fully removed from office because they felt he was
personally preventing them from making a financial
killing in cotton speculation.

Leaders among this group were:

> Jay Cooke
>> Philadelphia financier
>
> Henry Cooke
>> Washington banker
>
> Thurlow Weed
>> politician - journalist
>
> Robert D. Watson
>> cotton speculator, and
>
> Ward Hill Lamon
>> U.S. Marshall of Washington D.C."

And on page 216, the two authors listed other names that
were mentioned in the diary:

> Jefferson Davis
>> the head of the Southern Government and a
>> member of the Knights of the Golden Circle
>
> Judah P. Benjamin
>> Secretary of War, and then Secretary of
>> State in the Confederacy

Mr. Benjamin was an interesting man. A biography about him
written by Pierce Butler in 1980 states that:

"All biographers of Benjamin have confronted the
same problem, the absence of personal papers. In the
last hours of the Confederacy [1865] Benjamin and
his staff burned most of his papers." page xviii

The book entitled CONFEDERATE AGENT by James D. Hogan told its readers just what else those records contained:

"When Richmond, [Virginia, the capital of the South] was burning, Secretary of State Judah P. Benjamin burned the records of his and of Lines' [the Confederate agent who is the subject of the book] secret dealing with the Copperhead leaders." (Page 16)

On the preceding page, the author told his readers just who these "Copperheads" were:

"Copperhead was a catch-all phrase describing several secret societies [including] the Knights of the Golden Circle . . . and several others." (Page 15)

So Secretary Benjamin was a dedicated believer in the cause of the South. For instance, his biographer states:

"Mr. Benjamin, armed with personal letters from the Barings [a banking family] . . . wasted his summer vacation in 1859 in the effort to get financial aid in Europe." page 190

(One example of the power of the Baring banking family is given in this quote by Cardinal Richelieu, the French cleric and statesman, (1585 - 1642), who has been quoted as saying:

"There are six great powers in Europe: England, France, Russia, Austria, Prussia and the Baring Brothe's." (Quoted on pages 9 - 10 THE MERCHANT BANKERS by Joseph Wechsler.)

So here we see the connection between the Knights of the Golden Circle and the international bankers that had organ-iced the Knights as the organization committed to precipitating the Civil War. And Secretary Benjamin burned the records of this connection.

The Barings had come to the United States in 1783, when they opened a business in Philadelphia. In just 19 years, they had become so powerful in America that they financed the Louisiana Purchase by selling $11,250,000 in bonds to the Jefferson administration. (Page 81, THE MERCHANT BANKERS, by Wechsburg)

One well known author apparently agreed that Secretary Benjamin was successful in his "efforts to get financial aid in Europe. He called him:

"one of the financial wizards of the Confederacy."
(OUR CROWD, Stephen Birmingham, p 154)

And the reason was real: Secretary Benjamin not only had contacts with the Barings, he had other key contacts as well:

"Benjamin . . . was the Civil War campaign strategist of the House of Rothschild."THE FEDERAL RESERVE, Kennan, page 246)

So the South was largely financed by European bankers.

But, let me return now to the story of **John Wilkes Booth**.

Modern historians have now dug out the information that proves that **Booth** did not die in the barn as historians have recorded for over 100 years.

Booth was also a member of the Knights of the Golden Circle, and it is known that he knew that Jesse James had become the head of the organization after the war had ended. **Booth** traveled widely after his supposed death, and one of the cities he settled in was Granbury, Texas, the city where Dalton was later buried in 1951. (JESSE JAMES AND THE LOST CAUSE, page 149)

But **Booth** had a weakness for alcohol and he started drinking too heavily and was revealing his true identity, which was contrary to the oath of secrecy he had taken as a member of the Knights. Stories to this effect reached Jesse and he knew that he had to silence the assassin. He found **Booth** staying in a rooming house in Enid, Oklahoma, on January 13, 1903, 38 years after **Booth** had allegedly been shot in the barn.

James had been providing **Booth** with $300 a month to live on from the money of the Knights of the Golden Circle organization. (JESSE JAMES AND THE LOST CAUSE, page 150) But, as stated previously, **Booth** had taken an oath as a member of that organization that he would not reveal any of its secrets and that he would obey any command of any superior in the organization without question.

This is that oath:

> "I will solemnly keep all the secrets of the Golden Circle, and I will faithfully perform whatever I may be commanded."

J. Frank Dalton has told the world that he went to Enid and ordered **Booth** to drink two glasses of lemonade that Jesse had put arsenic into. Boyd drank the two glasses and died in the presence of Jesse. (JESSE JAMES AND THE LOST CAUSE, page 16.)

The owner of the rooming house went to **Booth**'s room several days later because he had not seen him, and found the body laying in his bed. He found that the body had mummified from the arsenic and that it would not have to be embalmed.

There is some evidence that Dalton's story about poisoning **John Wilkes Booth** might be true.

The Oklahoma City Daily Oklahoman newspaper published an article on this man's death. These are excerpts from that article:

> "Enid, Oklahoma, June 2, 1903: Further evidence is at hand that the man who died here last January and who was supposed by some to be **John Wilkes Booth** was really that man.
>
> He has been identified by [1] Junius Brutus Booth [the nephew of John Wilkes Booth,] [2] his brother, and [3]others who knew **Booth** during the war.
>
> After the death of the man here, certain papers found upon his person led to the opinion that he was the fugitive assassin supposed to have been killed 38 years ago."

Another article supported the claim, this one datelined St. Louis, Missouri, on June 2, 1903: a special from Enid, Oklahoma:

> ". . . in his [meaning David E. George, the alias of **John Wilkes Booth** at the time] effects was found a letter directed to K.L. Bates of Memphis, Tennessee. Mr. Bates came here at once and fully identified the body as **John Wilkes Booth**."

This K.L. Bates might have been Finis Bates, or a relative of his, the author of a book on **John Wilkes Booth** entitled THE ESCAPE AND SUICIDE OF JOHN WILKES BOOTH. This Bates wrote his book after he was called to George's room (**Booth** had been using the alias of John St. Helen in Granbury, Texas) in 1887 when **Booth** thought he was dying. This is how the Hood County News newspaper of June 21, 1997 covered this part of the story:

> "According to the legend [that **Booth** survived the shooting in the barn in Virginia] one time when he [**Booth**/George/St. Helen] became gravely ill in 1887 and thought he was dying, St. Helen confessed to Granbury [Texas] attorney Finis Bates that he was **Booth**.
>
> According to his (Mr. Bates') story, he had acted as Mr. **Booth**'s confidential advisor for nearly 40 years."

1903 minus the "nearly 40" years makes the first meeting between Bates and **Booth** to be about 1865. This makes it appear as if Bates and **Booth** first met each other about the same time as the assassination of Abraham Lincoln, and not at the 1877 meeting to discuss **Booth**'s confession. So there seems to be reasons to believe that **Booth** had sent for Bates in 1877 for reasons other than to hear his confession. In other words, Bates already knew that "George" was **Booth**, the assassin of Lincoln before he listened to his story. That seems to make sense out of this part of the **Booth** story.

So it appears as if this K.L. Bates might have been, in actuality, Finis L. Bates, the attorney who heard **Booth**'s "confession" in 1877, but who had known him since the Civil War. It certainly could be that K.L. Bates was the son of Finis Bates and he could have also visited with **Booth** with his father and known that he was **Booth** just as his father did. So it is possible that K.L. was the son of Finis Bates.

According to the story told by J. Frank Dalton, the body of "St. Helen/George" was taken on a tour of the United States after his death as an exhibition wherein the American people were encouraged to pay a fee to see the "body of **John Wilkes Booth**, the assassin of Abraham Lincoln." The reason that they could exhibit the body was because the arsenic had embalmed the body without any decay.

The Oklahoma City article pointed out that it was Bates himself who sent the mummy out on tour after the poisoning of **Booth**, and that his wife sold the body to a carnival after Mr. Bates had died.

LIFE magazine did a photographic feature on this mummy in it's July 11, 1938 issue.

The article accompanying the photographs in the Life article stated that doctors in 1938 had examined the mummy's LEFT leg and had discovered that it had been broken, just as reported by witnesses at the theater in 1865 after **Booth** jumped to the stage.

The Hood County News of June 21, 1997 printed an article that amplified these comments by Life. They reported that:

"A team of six physicians X-rayed the remains. The X-rays revealed that the mummy had a healed left ankle fracture and a deformed right thumb.

Booth had broken his left ankle when jumping from a theater balcony [Booth jumped from a box in the Ford's Theater in Washington D.C.] after shooting

166

President Lincoln.

The deformed thumb came after a stage accident that occurred during Booth's acting career.

The mummy's stomach also revealed a ring with the letter 'B.' Booth had reportedly swallowed it to escape recognition during his flight from the [Northern] troops."

So it appears as if history could have written the truth about the death of **John Wilkes Booth** had they only wished to do so. Just like many facts in this case, the truth was there for all those who cared enough to discover it themselves.

And if J. Frank Dalton is correct, Civil War historians will have to re-write major portions of their writings.

chapter fourteen
THE CIVIL WAR, Part 3

The Civil War has a secret side to it even beyond the details just written about.

And that is the Masonic involvement in the planning of it.

There are several clues that need to be explored to substantiate the claims that the Masons were directly involved in the planning of the war. And they are these:

1.   Mackey's Encyclopedia, written by **Albert G. Mackey**, 33rd Degree Mason, informed the reader that:

> "Charleston, South Carolina: it was there that the first [33rd Degree] Supreme Council of the Ancient and Accepted Scottish Rite was established in 1801."

The reason that this city was selected was because it was underneath the 33rd Degree Northern Latitude (one of the imaginary lines that parallel the equator.) So the 33rd Degree Northern Latitude has special symbolic significance to the Masons. That was why they selected this city to form their first 33rd Degree Council.

It was in Charleston, South Carolina that the first shot of the Civil War was fired, at a United States fort called Ft. Sumter, underneath the 33rd Degree Northern Latitude.

It would be appropriate at this time to suspend the discussion about the Civil War once again to add some comments regarding the involvement of the Masonic Lodge in the assassination of President John Kennedy on November 22, 1963, in Dealey Plaza, Dallas, Texas.

First of all, the location of the assassination is the key to the understanding of the Masonic involvement in it. Dallas is also underneath the 33rd Degree Northern Latitude, just like the city of Charleston, South Carolina.

Dealey Plaza has an obelisk in it, that has a plaque at its base that states that:

"Within this small park was built the first fraternal lodge."

The two words "fraternal lodge" certainly could refer to another civic organization, other than the Masons. But there are two reasons that I believe it referred to that organization:

1. The fact that this plaque referred to a "lodge." As far as I know it is only the Masons that refer to their buildings as "lodges."

2. The obelisk is especially significant to the Masons. The best evidence of this is that the Washington monument, built to honor George Washington, this nation's first President, is in the form of an obelisk.

    Pres. Washington was a very visible member of the Masons.

The day of the assassination was November 22. November is the 11th month of the year and that number, when added together to the 22 of the number of the day of the shooting, total 33.

Also, it was on November 22, 1307 that Pope Clement the 5th issued a Papal Bull exposing the Knights Templar Order and Jacques deMolay, its leader at the time. Later, on March 11, 1314, the Catholic Church burned brother deMolay at the stake. March is the 3rd month of the year and that times the 11th day equals 33 once again.

The Scottish Rite Masonic Lodge today is a descendent of the Knights Templar, and at the 30th of their 33 Degrees, the Scottish Rite Masons take an oath as follows:

> "We do most sacredly and solemnly vow, and to each other renewedly pledge our Masonic and Knightly Word, that we will, by all legal and honourable [the written ritual's spelling of the word] means, avenge the murderers of our predecessors of this Order . . . ."

That means the 30th Degree Mason takes an oath to avenge the murderers of Jacques deMolay, meaning the Catholic Church.

John Kennedy was this nation's first Catholic President.

2.   The Confederate flag consists of an "X" colored blue in a field of red. The "X" is slightly flattened, meaning the height is not equal to its width, with 13 stars inside the two bars of the "X."

If the number of stars represents the number of states that joined the Confederacy, there should have been only 11 stars, since only 11 states seceded. Those who claim that the South was waiting for two more states to join the Confederacy are incorrect since the flag was officially approved in 1863, about in the middle of the Civil War. So the number of stars on the flag do not signify the number of states in the Confederacy.

They have a symbolic meaning.

And the number 13 has special Masonic significance.

The April, 1960 edition of Masonic magazine called THE NEW AGE magazine reported that there were:

"Masonic Symbols In a $1 Bill:

such as:

> 13 leaves in the olive branches
> 13 bars and stripes in the shield
> 13 feathers in the tail
> 13 arrows
> 13 letters in 'E Pluribus Unum' on the ribbon
> 13 stars in the green crest above
> 13 granite stones in the Pyramid with the Masonic 'All-seeing Eye' completing it
> 13 letters in 'Annuit Coeptis,' meaning 'God has prospered.'"

I would like to explain that this interpretation of the two Latin words "ANNUIT COEPTIS" in the circle on the left side of our dollar bill is incorrect. These two circles, this one with the pyramid and the other with the eagle, constitute THE GREAT SEAL OF THE UNITED STATES, unanimously adopted in 1782, shortly after the Declaration of Independence established this nation, as that symbol of the United States.

The proper interpretation of these words is "ANNOUNCING THE BIRTH OF." The words on the bottom "NOVUS ORDO SECLORUM" are Latin for the words "NEW WORLD ORDER." So this nation's founding fathers were "ANNOUNCING THE BIRTH OF THE NEW WORLD ORDER" on July

4, 1776.

Lastly, this author has written a book to explain just what this NEW WORLD ORDER is and how it should be of concern to every American. That book is entitled THE NEW WORLD ORDER, and was completed about one year prior to President George Bush's mention of the phrase in a speech in 1990.

Now, back to the number 13.

The April 28, 1982 COIN WORLD magazine had another article confirming much of what the Masons just stated about the number 13. Their article was entitled "No. 13 important to Great Seal," and contained these additional 13's in our early history:

"George Washington [a visible member of the Masons until his death in 1799] had 12 generals around him for a total of 13;

'AN APPEAL TO GOD,' a famous slogan of the period, had 13 letters in it as did the equally famous 'DON'T TREAD ON ME' slogan;

The words 'July the Fourth' [the day that America's Founding Fathers declared their independence from England] total 13 letters;

13 arrows in the eagle's talon on one side;

13 leaves in the eagle's other talon;

The last two numbers of our year of independence, 1776, (the 7 + the 6) total 13;

The name of our National Bird, the AMERICAN EAGLE, has 13 letters in it;

A total of 13 people worked on the Great Seal;

A committee of 13 controlled this country's naval affairs between 1775 and 1785;

The first U S Navy had a fleet of 13 ships."

Another 13 is concealed inside the fact that the first American government was formed 13 years after the Declaration of Independence (1789 - 1776 = 13 years)

But one of the most hidden Masonic symbols is the one that conceals their involvement in designing the Great Seal of the United States.

The Seal has a six pointed star drawn above the head of the eagle. It consists of 13 five pointed stars drawn in such a way as to form a six pointed star.

When the observer draws a line through the 12 stars that form the six pointed star, excluding the one in the center, and then transfers that line drawing of the 6 pointed star to the Pyramid side of the Great Seal, and places it over the pyramid itself inside the letters forming the Latin phrase "ANNUIT COEP- TIS, NOVUS ORDO SECLORUM," (the triangle containing the eye becomes one of the points of the six pointed star it- self) the points of the star point to the following letters in the Latin phrase:

point # 1:	The "A" in ANNUIT,
point # 2:	a blank space above the "All-Seeing Eye",
point # 3:	The "S" in COEPTIS,
point # 4:	The "N" in NOVUS,
point # 5:	The 2nd "O" in ORDO, and
point # 6:	The "M" in SECLORUM.

The letters A - S - N - O - M are an ANAGRAM (defined as a word or phrase made from another by rearranging its letters) for the word MASON.

It is fair to conclude that the Masons had a major role in creating the Great Seal of the United States and concealing their involvement in symbols. They have also concealed their involvement in the formation of the American Government as well.

(If the reader wants additional information as to how the Masons amongst this nation's FOUNDING FATHERS, clearly in the majority of both the Signers of the Declaration of Independence, and the Constitution itself, created an "occult" (defined as hidden, concealed) nation, you might consider reading my booklet entitled AMERICA'S SECRET DESTINY (available on my website.) There is even more evidence inside to consider.)

The quotations taken from the major Masonic writers shown at the beginning of this book are real: the Masons are indeed "the invisible powers behind the thrones of earth."

Just as they claim.

chapter fifteen
THE SECOND CIVIL WAR

The period shortly after the Civil War is the period wherein Jesse James played a significant role. It is true that Jesse James had a minor role in the Civil War of 1861 to 1865, but he played a far more significant role in the period after the war had concluded.

Because the Knights of the Golden Circle that Jesse was head of after the war ended wanted to create a Second Civil War after the first one had failed to provide the bankers with their goal: the "central bank."

Modern day historians have often cited the slogan created by the Knights to encourage the South to provoke a second Civil war:

"THE SOUTH SHALL RISE AGAIN"

but do not explain what it meant.

This slogan was intended by the Knights to create the favorable conditions so that the South would want to start a second Civil War after the South had lost the first one. And the reason is simple: the bankers had not obtained their goal in the war, their central bank, so they were making a major attempt to create the conditions to force the United States into fighting another one.

Dalton himself explained that this was the strategy of the Knights in the book entitled JESSE JAMES AND THE LOST CAUSE (page 45):

". . . our efforts to promote another dreadful and bloody civil war in America."

He described:

"a fanatical plot was hatched by us to really put on a greater war than the first in the United States." (Page 45, JJ AND THE LOST CAUSE)

In 1867, after the war was over, the Knights of the Golden Circle, and certain members of the Masons, formed an auxiliary group, called the Ku Klux Klan, to start racial tension again over the still smoldering "black-white" issue. It is known that racial riots were started in several major cities in the South after the war and hundreds were shot or injured.

One author described those attempts with these words:

"Even more cruel was the persistent effort of soldiers to instill into the negro's mind a hatred of the men with whom he would have to live [obviously referring to the white people] after the army should march away.

The correspondent of 'The Nation' [apparently a magazine of the day] ascribed the labor and race relations to the bad influence of the negro's Northern friends, 'particularly soldiers.'

The soldiers [were] inciting the blacks against their former masters.

Emissaries of radicalism were constantly inflaming the freedmen . . . turning them against the native whites." (THE REVOLUTION AFTER LINCOLN,

It might be appropriate at this juncture to explain a little more about the Masonic Lodge and its involvement in the affairs of the United States. Because it is impossible to understand America's past without an understanding of the part played by this secret society.

It is an interesting fact that J. Frank Dalton, in the book entitled JESSE JAMES WAS ONE OF HIS NAMES, claimed to be a 33rd degree Mason (that is the highest known of their degrees. The majority of the Masons stop at the 3rd Degree, (and they are called BLUE LODGE MASONS) a small percentage go on to become 32nd Degree Masons but only a small percentage of these are invited into the honorary 33rd degree.) It is interesting to ponder whether or not the Masons knew that the man they had invited into their small circle of 33rd Degree Masons was in truth Jesse James, the famous outlaw, living under the alias of William Andrews Clark. (It is my opinion that they knew precisely who he was. They just would not admit it publicly.)

Henry J. Walker wrote about the year that Dalton had joined the Masonic Lodge. This is what he wrote on page 166:

> "Jesse had been associated with the Masonic Lodge since 1862."

It must be conceded that Mr. Walker was one of those who believed that J. Frank Dalton was the real Jesse James. And he had reason to believe that Mr. Dalton was a Mason.

One of the evidences of Jesse's masonic membership consists of the photograph of the two James brothers, Frank and Jesse, standing side by side, each giving a rather strange symbol with their right hands. Frank is giving the sign indicating that he was a Mason, and Jesse is giving the sign that he was a member of the Knights of the Golden Circle. So it would appear by this photograph that Jesse had as yet not joined the Masons, but that his brother Frank had. They appear to be in their 20's at the time that the picture was taken.

J. Frank Dalton claimed he was a 33rd Degree Mason so if he was in truth Jesse James, it may be concluded that he had joined the Masons after this photograph was taken in 1872.

It is also an interesting fact that William Daniel Mangam, in his book written about William Andrews Clark entitled THE CLARKS, AN AMERICAN PHENOMENON, states that Clark joined the Masons as early as 1865, after the Civil War, and was "elected to higher offices, and in 1877 became Grand Master of the Grand Lodge of Montana."

A 4 volume set of books entitled 10,000 FAMOUS FREE-MASONS by William R. Denslow, published by the Macoy Publishing & Masonic Supply Co. has this biographical sketch of Senator Clark:

"William A. Clark: (1839 - 1925) U.S. Senator from Montana, 1901 - 1907. Born Jan. 8, 1839 at Connellsville, Pa. He was grand master [the equivalent of their state-wide President] of the Grand Lodge of Montana in 1877. Died Mar. 2, 1925."

So William Andrews Clark, the alias of Jesse James, was a high ranking member of the Masonic Lodge.

The real Clark would have been 25 or 26 years of age in 1865 when he joined the Lodge, having been born in 1839. (There is a dispute, as I stated earlier, about the date Jesse joined the

Masons. The previous statement said he joined in 1862. I prefer the 1865 date.) The picture of Jesse and Frank seems to indicate that he had not joined the Masons as of 1872, because he was not giving the sign of the Masons as was Frank; he was giving the sign of the Knights of the Golden Circle.

Another Mason of importance was 33rd degree Mason **Albert Pike,** the Sovereign Grand Commander (the equivalent of their international President.) The statue of him in Washington D.C. claims that he was "the leader of the worldwide masonic movement," from 1859 to 1891. There is Masonic literature that states that Mr. Pike actually assisted in the formation of the Ku Klux Klan.

According to **Henry Coil**, yet another 33rd Degree Mason, in his MASONIC ENCYCLOPEDIA, **Albert Pike** "was the Chief Judicial Officer of the K.K.K. [meaning the Ku Klux Klan.]"

The founder of the Ku Klux Klan was Confederate Lt. General **Nathan Bedford Forrest**, another member of the Masonic Lodge.

It is worthy of notice at this time to point out that the Masons officially are strangely silent on the role of **Pike** and **Forrest** in the creation of the Ku Klux Klan.

The 33rd Degree Council has published a book entitled **ALBERT PIKE,** THE MAN BEYOND THE MONUMENT (meaning the statue of him in Washington D.C.) There are two items of interest in this book that I would like to mention.

1. On page 228 of the book, the Masons have written that "the **Albert Pike** Monument [meaning, once again, the statue] was approved by Congress in 1898

179

and completed in 1901, ten years after **Pike**'s death. So Congress approved a statue of a Confederate General, and the "Leader of the Worldwide Masonic Movement" to be placed in the nation's capital.

In my book, THE NEW WORLD ORDER, I discuss the evidence taken from their own literature that MASONRY IS A RELIGION. So Congress approved a statue of the LEADER OF THE WORLDWIDE MASONIC RELIGION, that would be placed in the capital.

So much for the "separation of church and state."

2.   It is interesting that this statue is the only one of a Confederate Army soldier in Washington D.C. (**Albert Pike** was a General in the Southern Army during the Civil War.)

This book is 254 pages long and is full of the writings and teachings of **Pike**, yet there is NOT ONE MENTION of his involvement in the K. K. K., nor is there any reference to **Nathan Bedford Forrest**, the Founder of the K. K. K., and **Pike**'s fellow Mason, inside the book.

Apparently the Masons are not interested in informing the people of American just how involved the Masons were in the founding of the Klan.

The Ku Klux Klan had an important purpose according to Dalton:

"The K K K was the secret military police of the Old South, directly under the domination and scrutiny of The Knights of the Golden Circle at all times." page
P. 47 JJ AND THE LOST CAUSE

"The treasurer and comptroller, who had sole and complete custody of all gold and silver bullion, money, jewels and taxations, was . . . me, Jesse Woodson James." Page 47, JJ AND THE LOST CAUSE.)

This admission on Dalton's part is extremely important, for reasons that I will discuss in later chapters of this book.

Jesse decided to join the Ku Klux Klan himself in 1867:

"It was right there, that we decided then and there that we would join the secret military police [the K K K] of the old Southland. That organization was the original Ku Klux Klan. Some of us were already members of the Knights of the Golden Circle." P. 58 JJ AND THE LOST CAUSE

The "Frank Dalton" who wrote for the CRITTENDEN MEMOIRS claimed that:

"The Ku Klux Klan was organized shortly after that and Cole and John Younger stayed in it till the spring of '67, when Bob and Jim joined them." (CRITTENDEN MEMOIRS , page 358)

So there is an interesting connection between Jesse James, the Masons, the Knights of the Golden Circle, The Ku Klux Klan and **Albert Pike**, in their desire to create a Second Civil War.

J. Frank Dalton told those chronicling his story that he and his gang were in the west during the period shortly after the war robbing trains, banks and stage coaches to raise money for the second civil war. He further claimed that he had buried over $7 billion in gold in the West, someday hoping to relocate it for removal to finance the second war. However, other historans have stated that Jesse's gang acquired no more than $175,000 (JESSE JAMES: THE MAN AND THE MYTH, page 3) in their various robberies so this larger sum of money had to come from another source, and the money belonging to the Knights of the Golden Circle would be the logical source of it.

But these efforts to start a second Civil War failed, and "THE SOUTH NEVER ROSE AGAIN," as least as the Knights and the Masons had envisioned. And there are reports that much of that gold is still buried in the United States. Dalton reported the location of approximately 100 of these depositories in the book entitled JESSE JAMES WAS ONE OF HIS NAMES. However, the list contains only a brief description of each location such as "Rocky Ford Treasure," so it is quite likely that the gold either is still buried at these sites, and will not be found by the treasure hunter, or has been removed by other members of the Knights.

But, there appears to have been media coverage of the discovery of one of these sites.

The television program called UNSOLVED MYSTERIES reported that a huge cache of "gold bars, coins and a crown" were found in White Sands, New Mexico, before it became a National Monument, back in the late 1940's. Robert Stack, the host of that program, reported that the U. S. government removed the contents of this cave. He ended this segment with this cryptic comment:

"This gold was either the gold of the Jesuits in the area, the gold of the indians, or Emperor [of Mexico] Maximilian's treasure."

It seems unlikely that the indians or the Jesuits would have created a "crown" out of this gold, and far more likely that this was the treasure of the Emperor. The "crown" could have been the one that graced his head as he led the nation of Mexico.

J. Frank Dalton reported that he and his gang assisted the Emperor in leaving Mexico in 1867 with his fortune, and it is conceivable that Mr. Stack was right: the gold and the golden crown were from the Emperor's treasure, buried in New Mexico by Jesse and his gang after they brought the Emperor out of Mexico.

It has been reported by historians that the Emperor died in Mexico, but Dalton reported that he and others from the Knights brought him out of Mexico to the safety of America.

So it is unlikely that this list of treasure sites will be of any help to the treasure hunter.

The plans of the bankers had failed: there was no second Civil War.

It was now time to change their strategy.

chapter sixteen
THE NEW STRATEGY: ARTIFICIAL PANICS

It is at this point that I must stop my reporting on the American past, and continue with my discussion of the powers these central banks have.

As I mentioned before, no banking system anywhere in the world has enough money in the bank at any one time to meet the immediate cash demands of all of its depositors if they all came in for their cash at the same time. The reason is clear: the money they deposited has been loaned out and is in the hands of the borrowers. In fact, it more than likely is not in their hands either: they have used the loan to pay off their debts and even these individuals do not have the money either: they have used the money to pay off their debts.

In other words, if all of the depositors went to their bank at the same time to withdraw their money, the bank would simply not have enough cash to meet all of those demands. (The banks keep about 10 to 20% of the deposits on hand to meet expected withdrawals: about 80 to 90% has been loaned out.)

When this happens, it is called a "bank run."

So the bank planners decided that if they could artificially cause a "bank run," they could use the difficult times the event caused to accuse the state chartered banks of causing the problem..

The bankers then could offer the people the solution to prevent these events from happening in the future: a Central Bank.

And true to their word, they caused "bank runs" in 1873, 1893, and 1907. (By the way, each of these "runs" were planned during the time that Jesse James, the banker, was alive. He certainly could have learned their techniques while he was personally in the banking business. In fact, it is easily conceivable that he helped formulate them, at least the later ones.)

The Panic of 1907 might serve as a model.

The nation's leading banker at that time was J.P. Morgan (today it is David Rockefeller. The two men play the same role: they are the banking expert that we are all supposed to listen to. When Morgan spoke, the American people listened!)

Mr. Morgan visited London, England and Paris, France in 1907 (the homes of two of the Rothschild banking family were in London and Paris. John T. Flynn in his book MEN OF WEALTH, page 98, wrote:

"In 1815 they [meaning the Rothschild banking family] were the bankers for the British government."

They had other offices in the major cities of Europe.) The reasons for his visits to these cities is not commonly known, but I believe it was because he went there to discuss his plans on causing the artificial "bank run" of 1907. Whatever plans he made for America would certainly affect Europe, and it is presumed that these bankers discussed what results they could expect from this contrived occurrence.

When Mr. Morgan returned to America, he announced that a

particular bank in New York was insolvent. The people, told to believe this banker by the media, believed him and rushed to this bank to withdraw their funds, and, exactly as predicted by Morgan, the bank proved to be insolvent. As I said, no bank has enough cash on hand at any one time to meet the demands of all of its depositors. It followed that the people in other parts of the United States, believing that J.P. Morgan knew what he was talking about because what he had predicted came true, reasoned that if he was right about that bank, there might be reasons that their particular local bank could be insolvent as well.

So people all over America went to their banks at the same time, thereby causing a nation-wide bank run. The "bank insolvency" that Morgan commented on was not just one bank, it was many banks! In fact, the panic was nationwide!

Then Mr. Morgan offered his solution: America must create a central banking system that would take the control of the banking system away from these "unscrupulous" state chartered bankers who had "mismanaged the affairs of their respective banks." So he and the other American banker conspirators offered America their solution: The Private Reserve!

The law creating the Private Reserve was passed in 1913, and the European (and now American) bankers had accomplished their task. It had taken them 137 years, three major wars, and three major bank runs, but they were about to fulfill their goal: they were about to create a permanent central bank with the passage of the Private Reserve Bill..

America now had a privately owned central banking system, with the power to print paper money out of nothing, back it with a promise of the government to redeem it with nothing, and then loan it to the government at interest. The government then declared that the money was "Legal Tender," which meant that the American people would have to accept it in everyday trade.

The trap had been sprung.

And the American people were caught in it.

The bankers had won, and the American people had lost!

Just as it was planned!

chapter seventeen
THE STORY CONTINUES

Once the reader understands Central Banking, America's past starts to make sense. And Jesse's involvement in it becomes clearer.

So, with that understanding, let me return to the story of J. Frank Dalton.

Mr. Dalton was claiming that Jesse James had not died on April 3, 1882. He was claiming that he was the famous outlaw and he continued making that claim until his death on August 15, 1951.

And, as has been discussed earlier in this book, stories started circulating shortly after the funeral that Jesse had not been shot in St. Joseph. As already discussed, the Liberty, Missouri Tribune reported that sightings of Jesse had started only 11 days after Jesse had been buried.

But generally the American people did not believe the stories, because to do so required them to accept a distasteful conclusion: others had to be involved in the fraud as well, and the Tribune reported just what that meant:

Such a conclusion would implicate:

> "Mrs. James [actually the widow of Charlie Bigelow, if Mr. Dalton is right] Mrs. [Zarelda, his mother] Samuel, Governor **[Thomas] Crittenden**, Sheriff [James R.] Timberlake, [Kansas City] Police Commissioner [Henry H.] Craig and others in a scheme of

fraud and perjury." P. 169 JESSE JAMES WAS HIS NAME by William A. Settle Jr.

It might be recalled that Dalton was claiming that **T.T. Crittenden** and he were boyhood friends from their youthful days in Kentucky.

One possible evidence that **Crittenden** and Jesse were indeed friends comes from Rudy Turilli's book on page 25. This is what he reports:

> "In 1937, a book was published by Henry Huston Crittenden, the son of **Thomas T. Crittenden**, Governor of Missouri in 1882. This book is called the 'CRITTENDEN'S MEMOIRS.'"

As I reported earlier, Mr. Crittenden selected J. Frank Dalton to write some 20 pages on the life of Jesse James to complete the memoirs of the Governor.

It could be argued that this is further evidence that J. Frank Dalton was the real Jesse James, because the man who wrote this chapter was named "Frank Dalton."

But there are others who stepped forward to claim that Dalton was the real Jesse.

After his story went public in 1948, hundreds of citizens came forward to Lawton, Oklahoma to talk to the old man and see if he was in truth the famous outlaw. Many of these witnesses signed notarized statements testifying that they personally knew that J. Frank Dalton was who he claimed to be.

In a book entitled JESSE JAMES WAS ONE OF HIS NAMES, by Del Schrader and Jesse James III, (there are some who question whether the second individual was a relative of Jesse Woodson James, but he claimed that he was) the two authors list 42 signed and notarized affidavits that witnesses signed claiming that J. Frank Dalton was indeed Jesse Woodson James. These included reports from cousins, friends, reformed outlaws, employees, fellow Confederate soldiers, relatives of friends, ex-outlaws, gang members, lawmen including a Chief of Police, and a minister.

A typical affidavit read:

> "My father knew Jesse W. James and J. Frank Dalton has answered my questions correctly. I am convinced he is the real Jesse W. James."

The Lawton Constitution of June 2, 1948 offered its readers this testimony:

> "Another Lawtonian today had joined the swelling tide of believers in the authenticity of J. Frank Dalton's claim that he is the original Jesse James.
>
> 'I asked the old man [Dalton] ... and he answered all my questions to my complete satisfaction. Nobody but Jesse James could have answered some of them.'"

These unsolicited testimonies by people close to Jesse James meant that probably there were thousands more who would have made similar statements about his veracity if they had been afforded the opportunity.

One of the more famous individuals making one of these testimonies was a famous woman of the "old west" known as Calamity Jane. She quoted a letter she had written on November 30, 1889 in her book entitled CALAMITY JANE'S

DIARY AND LETTERS that read:

"I met up with Jesse James not long ago. You know that he was killed in 1882 [7 years before the date of their meeting.] His mother swore that the body that was in the coffin was his, but it was another man.

He is passing under the name of Dalton but he couldn't fool me. I knew all the Daltons and he sure ain't one of them.

He told me he promised his gang and his mother that if he lived to be a hundred, he would confess."

Jane's testimony about Jesse's desire to tell the truth when he reached 100 needs to be partially corrected. Dalton claimed later that the reason he came forward when he was 100 years of age was because he and the other remaining members of the Knights promised each other that the one who reached 100 first would tell the truth about their activities.

Someone else who offered his statement that Dalton was in truth Jesse James was another famous outlaw of that period: William H. Bonney, better known as Billy the Kid. History has recorded that Billy had been shot at the age of 22, on July 4, 1881, by Sheriff Pat Garrett in Ft. Sumner, New Mexico. But in fact, Billy lived a full life until he died in 1951, as "Brushy Bill" Roberts and claimed he had lived next door to Jesse for six years of his life. And it has been recorded that both of these men knew the other man's secret.

It is an interesting sidelight to Billy's story that history has recorded that Sheriff Garrett never collected the reward money for Billy's death after he had allegedly shot him. (JESSE JAMES AND THE LOST CAUSE, page 136) It is quite possible that Garrett didn't want to defraud the government of the money because he, of all people, knew that he had not killed Billy the Kid.

The possibility that Billy the Kid never died in 1881 received some confirmation in 1987 when several townspeople in Hico, Texas said they had compiled evidence that one of their neighbors, Ollie L. "Brushy Bill" Roberts, was in truth the individual known as Billy the Kid.

An article that appeared nationwide stated that they had created a plaque that read, in part:

> "He spent the last days of his life trying to prove to the world his true identity and obtain the pardon promised him by the governor of the state of New Mexico. We believe his story."

The article reported that Bob Hefner, a local Justice of the Peace, had said that new evidence to support "Brushy Bill's" claims included the discovery of an empty grave where Billy was supposedly buried in Fort Sumner; affidavits from six people who claimed to have known Billy and Roberts as the same person; similar physical descriptions of the two; and Roberts' detailed knowledge of a New Mexico cattleman's power struggle in which his employer was ambushed. It has been reported that it was Billy's involvement in trying to avenge the death of a rancher who had employed him that got him involved in later waging a campaign to clear his name.

In their book JESSE JAMES WAS ONE OF HIS NAMES, the authors have reproduced a photograph of the old Dalton laying in his bed, and the man standing beside the bed is a man that the authors claim is Billy the Kid.

192

So two of this nation's most famous outlaws, Jesse James and Billy the Kid both lived past their recorded deaths, and both ended up supporting the claims of the other that they had lived past that time.

If both of these stories are true, parts of the story of "The Old West" have to be rewritten.

chapter eighteen
A SILENT PROTEST

One of the people who could have accepted or rejected J. Frank Dalton's claims that he was Jesse James was Robert James, the son of Jesse's brother, Frank James. Author Joe Wood detailed how Robert refused to see J. Frank Dalton when specifically asked to do so in his booklet entitled MY JESSE JAMES STORY.

Mr. Wood reports that he and Rudy Turilli, another of those who spent time with Dalton while he was alive between the years of 1948 and 1951, both felt that Robert would be the ideal person to reject or accept Dalton's claims. This is how Mr. Wood reported it:

> "The person [who had] come forward and exposed the previous imposters was Bob James, the son of Frank James, and Jesse's nephew."

"The previous imposters" exposed by Bob James were men who had claimed to be "the real Jesse James." One of the books that I read stated that there had been a total of 12 of these men, and apparently Robert James was quick to meet with some of them if not all of them to prove that they were imposters.

So they took their thoughts to J. Frank Dalton and Mr. Wood reported his response when he was told of their desire to contact Robert, his nephew.

Dalton was asked if he would like to see "his nephew" and he responded:

"Of course I would, but you will just be wasting your time. Bob will never agree to see you, but you go ahead. It will be a very interesting experience for you."

Before these two men, Mr. Wood and Rudy Turilli, left to visit with Robert James, they talked to Lester Dill, their friend and the owner of Meramec Caverns in Missouri, a place that the James gang often visited as a hideout during the days when they robbed banks. Mr. Dill provided the pair with a check for $10,000, and told them that they could offer it to Robert as an inducement to visit with Mr. Dalton.

I must be fair and point out that Mr. Dill had a commercial venture, his ownership in the Meramec Caverns that he charged an admission price to see, that would presumably receive a financial benefit if Frank's son would confirm that Dalton was Jesse James. So he certainly could have had an ulterior motive in offering to pay $10,000 to Robert James to see Mr. Dalton. But, in a free enterprise economy, this would be a normal business offer that would benefit both parties involved. Making a profit on a business is the engine that drives the FREE ENTERPRISE SYSTEM. So, Mr. Dill certainly could have wanted to increase attendance by getting a confirmation that Jesse James had visited his caverns.

Mr. Wood reported what Robert James said when the three of them met:

"Gentlemen, I want to make it very clear -- I will not see this man under any circumstances."

Mr. Wood asked this question later in his book:

"Why did he refuse $10,000 just to visit Uncle Jesse

for a short time?"

Readers can come up with their own answer and I am not certain that I have one. But it is very apparent that he did not want to meet J. Frank Dalton. So Robert James did not dispute nor accept the claim made by J. Frank Dalton that he was his uncle when he could have cleared up this matter once and for all.

But unfortunately for history, he chose not to.

And no one that I am aware of has attempted to offer an explanation.

chapter nineteen
WILLIAM ANDREWS CLARK

J. Frank Dalton reported that during his 103 years, he concealed his identity under a total of 72 aliases. That list consists of the following names: (in alphabetic order)

Col. Jesse Allsworth, Col. J. Alvord, Johnny Baker, Jim Barnhill, John M. Burke, William Campbell, Col. Sam Carey, Col. Ben Carr, Ben Carstairs, Joe Jesse Chase, Ben Clark, Edgar Clark, E.W. Clark, W.H. Clark, Wilbur Clark, Jesse Cole, William Cole, J.J. Corley, Jim Crow, George Curtis, Happy Jack Dalton, John Dalton, Col. J. Frank Dalton, Col. J.W. Edwards, J.W. Ely, Henry Ford, Col. John Franklin, Jesse Gates, J.W. Gates, "Bet a Million" Gates, Col. J.W. Harris, Jack Halbrook, Charles Havard, John Henry, "Big Bush" Hopkins, Charles Howard, John Davis Howard, Ray Huett, Col. Roy Hewitt, T.L. Jackson, Franklin James, Jes F. James, J.H. James, Jay James, John Jefferson, John Kerry, Charles Langdon, Charles Lawson, Robert E. Lee Lane, Col. Jack McClary, Col. Jesse McLoud, Col. Jesse McDaniels, Jim McDaniels, D.H. Moffat, Hank Moffat, W.J. Moffat, Col. Owens, Jim Putnam, Jesse Redman, Jesse Redmond, Dick Reed, Jim Reed, Sgt. Lawrence Schofield, Col. Stallsworth, J.W. St. Myers, Capt. Harrison Trow, Tom Vaughn, W.W. Wade, Capt. Felix Warren, Jesse Wilson, and Bruce Younger

But the most important alias that Jesse assumed is the name of:

It is the opinion of this writer that this was Jesse's most important alias.

If J. Frank Dalton is correct about his use of this alias, then enormous parts of the story about "the Old West" will have to be rewritten.

Because William Andrews Clark was one of the major figures in American history during the period after the Civil War. In fact, he was described by Senator **Robert M. LaFollette** of Wisconsin as being "one of a hundred men who own America." (THE WAR OF THE COPPER KINGS, C.B. Glasscock, page 42)

William Daniel Mangam, for 30 years the general business agent for one of the sons of William Andrews Clark, put it a little differently. He said that Mr. Clark was:

"One of the hundred men who ruled America." (Page 164 of THE CLARKS)

Either way, it is clear that Clark was a major player in this nation's past.

There was a real person by the name of William Andrews Clark. He was born on January 8, 1839 in Connelsville, Pennsylvania to John and Mary (maiden name: Andrews) Clark. (page 7, THE CLARKS.) In 1856, when young William was 17, the family moved to Van Buren County, Iowa and built a new farm in the fertile land there. (Page 8, THE CLARKS)

And after entering a teacher's school in Birmingham, Iowa, young William left Iowa in 1859 and moved to Missouri and became a teacher. (page 9, THE CLARKS) A book entitled THE WILLIAM A. CLARK COLLECTION, about the art collection that Mr. Clark left to the Corcoran Gallery, has a biography of Senator Clark that includes the locations where the young Clark taught:

> "From 1859 to 1860, he taught in the public schools of Pettis and Cooper Counties in Missouri."

These two counties are east of Kearney, Missouri, the city where Jesse James grew up. Pettis is the closer at about 60 miles away, and Cooper County is about 80 to 100 miles away. So it is certainly feasible that young Clark met the young James in the period between the years of 1859 to 1860.

(None of the books I was able to find on William Andrews Clark identified the city where Clark went to teach. However, J. Frank Dalton claimed that he "once taught school in Missouri, at Calico Rock." (JESSE JAMES RIDES AGAIN, page 33) But this quotation does not give any dates as to when this occurred.

Secondly, I have been unable to locate Calico Rock in Missouri, after checking with various universities and historical societies in that state. There is a Calico Rock in Arkansas, but it is doubtful that Jesse, a Missourian by birth, would admit to working in a city in Missouri when it was in truth in Arkansas. But it is possible that Jesse had taught in this town, because the city is near the border of Missouri and Arkansas.

But if Jesse never taught in a Missouri city, it is conceivable that he made this story up as being his way of identifying himself as the real William Andrews Clark.

It is my opinion that Jesse James assumed the identity of the real William Andrews Clark and lived under that, and other, aliases for about 89 years.

And I shall endeavor to provide my theories as to how that came about in the following chapters.

chapter twenty
THE SWITCH

Those who claim that Jesse James became William Andrews Clark are constantly pressed for an answer to the question: when did the switch take place? When did Jesse assume the name and identity of Clark?

It is the opinion of this writer that the transfer took place in 1862 or 1863.

A website called BOOKRAGS (www.bookrags.com) that features biographies of many well known people, has one on WILLIAM ANDREWS CLARK that says that "at the outbreak of the Civil War, Clark enlisted in an Iowa regiment."

I think it can be fairly presumed that Mr. Clark joined a NORTHERN unit, not a SOUTHERN one, since Iowa did not secede from the union to join the Confederacy, and that his place of birth was Pennsylvania, certainly a northern state.

The biography continues with this comment: "Discharged in 1862, he moved to Colorado Territory."

It has been claimed by Clark biographers that sometime in "the autumn of 1862," the real Clark left Missouri by driving a team of horses west to the territory of Colorado. (Page 10, THE CLARKS.) This certainly confirms the biography published by BOOKRAGS. He reportedly ended up as a gold miner on a hill near Denver, Colorado.

I can find no explanation as to how Clark could have been "discharged" after serving only a few months. It would seem reasonable that he was injured and given a medical discharge.

Both biographies then claim that in 1863, he left Colorado and journeyed to a more prosperous gold mine near Bannack, Montana, and it is here that the fabled wealth of the later Clark was acquired. At least that is what one of the Clark biographers has written. It is the opinion of this writer that this is when the "switch" took place, after Clark left Missouri to go to Colorado. Either Clark returned to Missouri after being "discharged in 1862," or Jesse visited Clark in the mining camps of Colorado. I prefer to believe that Clark returned to visit Missouri and that was when the switch took place.

The book entitled FRANK AND JESSE by Ted Yeatman gives another possible date:

"Jesse James probably joined the guerillas in the spring of 1864."

If this date of Jesse joining Bloody Bill Anderson's guerilla band is correct, Jesse joined the guerillas AFTER he went to Bannack, Montana. But this date would indicate that the switch had already taken place before his trip to Bannack.

The reason the switch had to take place before "Clark's" trip to Bannack is because people would remember him as Clark on any subsequent visit to that city. If the real Clark went to Bannack in 1863, and then Jesse returned to Bannack in 1864 or later as Clark, people in that city would know that he was an imposter and question what had happened to the real Clark.

The transfer had to take place before 1863 if that is the date of the first Clark visit to Montana. In other words, it had to be Jesse himself making that first visit to Bannack in 1863, so that when he returned, people there would recognize him.

There is reason to connect Jesse with the real Clark and that is in their genealogy.

J. Frank Dalton stated that his grandmother was a woman named Mary Andrews on his mother's side, and young Clark stated that his mother was a woman named Mary Andrews. (That must be where William's middle name, Andrews, came from.)

It seems to be too much of a coincidence that both men had a female relative named Mary Andrews. Is it possible that both men were related through the Andrews family? Is it possible that the two women named Mary Andrews were mother and daughter? Or even the same woman? Is it possible that the mother named her daughter after herself?

It is a common practice for a father to name a son after himself, but far less common for a mother to name a daughter after herself. However that does not mean that it doesn't happen. My grandmother told me she knew several women who had been named after their mother.

As I stated previously, this writer is of the opinion that Jesse James and William Andrews Clark were cousins through the Andrews family connection. And when William left Iowa for Missouri, he went there to find the James family because they were relatives. When he became a teacher, he might have been as close as 60 miles and as far away as about 100 miles away from the James family in Kearney.

If this is true, and that William was a believer in the cause of the North in the Civil War instead of a "rebel" as his biography states, then it is conceivable that Jesse could have killed him in 1862 or thereabouts because Jesse was strongly pro-South and anti-North. It does not take much imagination to picture an argument between the two cousins, one strongly pro-South and the other strongly pro-North, about the Civil War then being waged.

Frank James, Jesse's brother, had joined **Quantrill**'s Raiders before these events, and this group was fighting for the South.

It is well established that young Jesse had been badly beaten in May of 1863 (Yeatman, page 383) by a group of Northern soldiers who were looking for Frank James and/or **Quantrill**'s Raiders prior to his possible meeting date with William Clark.

According to the story, Jesse refused to tell the soldiers and they beat him, bayonetted him, and then burned his feet to get him to reveal the truth. Many feel that Jesse joined Bloody Bill Anderson's group after this event because he wanted to seek revenge against "those Yankees."

(It is interesting that the post-mortem on the body of J. Frank Dalton done after his death on August 17, 1951, showed that "both feet show evidence of having been severely burned.")

If Clark had returned to Missouri after his "discharge" from the Iowa regiment, and had stated a strong belief in the cause of the North in the war, it could have been cause for Jesse to strike back against him out of anger and contempt.

If he had done this, and killed Clark, it is conceivable that Jesse could have assumed the identity of William to silence those who couldn't locate William after that day. If anyone suspected that Jesse had killed him, they would have demanded that the sheriff find him and bring him to justice. It would have been reasonable for Jesse to have spread a story that William had left the area to become a gold miner and then assumed William's identity at his new location so that he could leave the area without being tried for the murder. Jesse's disappearance could have been explained by a statement that he had joined Anderson's gang, and after he had told others that William had left the area to become a gold miner.

There would be a period of time when Jesse continued living in Kearney after the killing of Clark in 1862, before he joined Anderson's guerilla army, and it must be presumed that people started wondering what had happened to Clark. Perhaps this questioning convinced Jesse that he had to leave his home to get away from the authorities who might have been looking for Clark.

Jesse then would have to have someplace to hide Jesse while he assumed the identity of Clark. So he claimed he had joined Anderson's army as Jesse, while he went to Colorado to assume the identity of Clark.

There is one more possibility to this switching and that is that these dates are in error, simply because of the conflicting stories being told by so many different people at the time.

So this is the best I can do with details that might not be true.

But if Jesse assumed the identity of a REAL WILLIAM AN-DREWS CLARK, a switch HAD to take place, or Dalton's story totally falls apart.

(One thought: one can only wonder what would have been the consequences of a sheriff going to "Bloody Bill" Anderson's guerilla army and make an attempt to arrest Jesse James for the murder of William Andrews Clark. I think it would be fair to conclude that "Bloody Bill" would not have allowed that arrest to occur. It would also be presumed that any law officer would have known it would be difficult if not impossible to arrest Jesse as well.)

This would explain the sudden decision on the part of Clark, the discharged Northern soldier, to become Clark, the Colorado "miner," and then to become a Montana copper miner, after he had been trained as a teacher and had actually secured employment as one. It would also explain the decision of Jesse to leave his farm and become a member of Anderson's guerilla army at about the same time.

The latest date the switch could have taken place appears to be "May of 1863" when Clark and three other men left their diggings in Colorado on a trip to Bannack, Montana where they had been told there were rich gold deposits. That is the date assigned to this trip by the Clark family biographers.

That date would seem to be the other end of the period when James and Clark could have "switched," because this is when Clark made his appearance in Montana where he would later make an enormous fortune in the copper industry. It must be presumed that the "switch" could not have occurred any time after May or June of 1863 for the reason already discussed: people in Montana would have noticed the change in his physical appearance after the two had switched identities if the switch had occurred after Clark had visited Montana.

So, in my scenario, the "switch" took place between 1862 and 1863.

The writer is aware that there is no direct evidence that this switch happened at this time, but is only offering a possible explanation of the fact that one of the two disappeared to "join Bloody Bill Anderson's guerilla organization" and the other "left teaching to become a miner" at about the same time.

In the absence of contrary evidence, this writer is going to stick to his assumptions because it seems to explain the rather strange circumstances of the situation.

chapter twenty-one
CLARK'S MONEY

The biographers of William Andrews Clark reported that he went home to Connelsville, Pennsylvania in March of 1869 and married a young woman named Katherine Stauffer from his home town. The reports are that after their wedding, he brought his bride to Montana.

The town hall in Clarkdale, Arizona, where Clark built a copper smelter to process the ore from his mine in Jerome, Arizona, has a photograph of Mr. Clark alongside one of his wife, Katherine Stauffer Clark. They claim that she died in 1893.

This is a rather difficult situation to explain because if this is true, my scenario about Jesse assuming the identity of William some five or six years before becomes difficult to explain. It is possible, of course, that Jesse did indeed marry a woman named Katherine Stauffer and claimed that he had done so in Connelsville because he needed to further establish the fact that he was William Andrews Clark.

No one today knows for certain, so this writer can only offer it as another puzzling bit of this incredible story.

Once again, reporting on this story is like walking in a fog with blinders on!!

In the book entitled JESSE JAMES WAS ONE OF HIS NAMES, the authors make the statement that Jesse married probably eight or ten women and one of them could have been Katherine Stauffer.

During this time, Senator William Andrews Clark continued accumulating his wealth. He built the San Pedro (California), Los Angeles, and Salt Lake City (Utah) Railroad. His wealth at that time was so enormous that he financed it himself, without placing any stocks or bonds on the market for sale to the public. In fact, some have written that it was the largest privately financed railroad in this nation's history. (No doubt it was some of the money from the Knights of the Golden Circle that financed the railroad. The reader will recall the statement Dalton made about the money of the Knights, as reported in JESSE JAMES AND THE LOST CAUSE, page 47):

> "The treasurer and comptroller, who had sole and complete custody of all gold and silver bullion, money, jewels and taxations, was me, Jesse Woodson James!"

So it is entirely conceivable that Clark used the money from the Knights to finance not only this railroad but his entire financial empire as well.

Author Herbert V. Young confirmed this with this comment from his book entitled GHOSTS OF CLEOPATRA HILL, a book about Clark's copper mine in Jerome, Arizona:

> ". . . Clark established no partnerships or financial liasons outside of his own family. He allowed no shares in any of his many corporations to be distributed to the public. He issued no bonds or mortgages."

Of course, if he was truly Jesse James, he would not have wanted a partner of his or individuals on a board of directors of some corporation that he might own to ask embarrassing questions about his past. Nor would he wish for stockholders to want information about him.

The railroad that Clark built went through the then very small community of Las Vegas, Nevada. The town was so small that the census of 1890 counted only thirty residents who had made permanent homes there.

Clark bought a large ranch in the area in 1902 that had water rights, so that he would have abundant water for his steam-powered engines.

And on May 15, 1905, he parceled off a piece of the desert for the city known as Las Vegas, and he laid out the streets for the city. He then sold lots to the general public. Interest was reportedly high for the land because of the arrival of Jesse's railroad, and the town of Las Vegas, Nevada was born.

Clark sold his interest in the railroad in 1921, thus ending his personal ventures in the state of Nevada.

However, in 1909, the county in which Las Vegas is situated and is the county seat of, was created out of Lincoln County, the county to its north, and the name the founders of the new county chose was Clark County, named after William Andrews Clark, the alias of Jesse James.

So Jesse James was a major player in the history of Las Vegas, the gambling capital of the west.

Clark became a visible figure in the copper industry in Montana after he first appeared in that state in 1863. His interests in the state made him a very wealthy individual. This is how the book entitled THE WAR OF THE COPPER KINGS put it: (page 120):

"Clark was a mining magnate with personal control of some of the richest mines in Butte, a banker with interests extending throughout the state, great lumbering interests around Plains and St. Regis on the slopes of the Bitter Root Mountains, smelting interests in the Butte area and Colorado, and control of the vast resources of the newly developed United Verde copper deposits in Arizona [the mine in Jerome.]

He owned the local streetcar system of Butte, and was reaching out toward tremendous water-power resources of Montana.

He was becoming a figure in the economic affairs of the nation."

(It is interesting that when J. Frank Dalton appeared in Lawton, Oklahoma in 1948, the newspapers reported that the reason he came was because he wanted to "travel again over the old trail." (Lawton Constitution, May 19, 1948, page 7) The newspaper then reported that the "trail led throughout Texas, Arkansas, Oklahoma, Kansas, Nebraska, the Dakotas, and on up into MONTANA." (Page 1, LAWTON CONSTITUTION.) But the newspaper did not explain why this "trail" led to Montana, the home of William Andrews Clark.)

There is a similar clue in the book written by Ted Yeatman. He wrote that Frank James also visited the state of Montana, and I am arguing that it was because he went there to see his brother Jesse, living under the alias of William Andrews Clark. He wrote:

"The president [**Teddy Roosevelt**, 1901 - 1909] . . . wanted to meet Frank, but the former outlaw was in Montana at the time."

211

The author does not make it clear when exactly this meeting was to take place, but it appears to have been in 1903. Nor does he say why Frank would have a reason to visit Montana. But if Jesse was in fact Clark, it would make sense: this was a brother visiting a brother.

These are other tantalizing clues that Dalton was William Andrews Clark who made a good percentage of his fortune in Montana. As far as I have determined, none of the reported James bank or train robberies were in Montana, so these curious references to Montana do not seem to fit unless the two individuals were referring to the time that Jesse spent in that state as William Andrews Clark.)

The United Verde Mine that Clark owned in Jerome, Arizona, mentioned above, came as a result of a lucky break in Clark's life.

Perhaps the next most important date in his life came in 1878 when he was selected to be the commissioner from Montana to the World's Exposition in New Orleans. This was a fortunate appointment for him, because while he was examining various mineral exhibits at the exposition, his attention was drawn to specimens of copper ore from the United Verde mine in Jerome, Arizona.

Clark visited the mine in 1888, and later started buying up shares of United Verde stock. Before a year was out, he owned 70% of the stock and he claimed that he made over $50,000,000 in profits from it during his time of ownership. Clark's biographer called this mine "his richest possession," (page 81, THE CLARKS) and one can certainly see why.

A report published by the town of Clarkdale, Arizona, the town that Mr. Clark created when he needed to build a copper smelter for his mine, reported in their Historical Resource Survey that:

"Clark had the money to develop the United Verde into one of the largest copper mines in the world."

Just as in the case of the railroad that James built, it is certainly conceivable that the money he used to buy the stock came from the money of the Knights of the Golden Circle.

The profits made from this mine (the mine closed all operations in 1953, many years after Clark had passed away) and from the other holdings of Clark made him an extremely wealthy man. Author Herbert V. Young said

". . . At the peak of his operations his holdings were worth no less than three hundred millions. Other estimators have claimed he was worth up to half a billion. He was classed by Senator **Robert La Follette** as among the hundred capitalists who ruled America, and Bernard Baruch [a close friend of Pres. **Franklin Roosevelt**] once named him as one of America's richest twelve." (GHOSTS OF CLEOPATRA HILL, MEN AND LEGENDS OF OLD JEROME)

But these estimates of Dalton/James' wealth are tame compared to those made in the book JESSE JAMES WAS ONE OF HIS NAMES. This is what the two authors reported:

"What was the old man's worth when he died in 1951? Relatives closest to him say the figure was somewhere between $1 billion and $2 billion with one estimate as high as $10 billion." (Page 97-98)

A sizeable fortune for a farmer from Missouri!

chapter twenty-two
WILLIAM ANDREWS CLARK, U.S. SENATOR

William Andrews Clark's attention soon turned to civic affairs, when in 1889, while Montana was still a territory, he served as president of the Montana Constitutional Convention. This meeting led to Montana being admitted to the union of the United States later that year.

In 1890, Clark announced his candidacy as a Democrat for the Senate of the United States from his home state of Montana. He was not successful in his attempt, and waited until 1893 when he again announced his candidacy for the Senate. Prior to the passage of the 17th Amendment to the Constitution of the united States of America in 1913, which called for the direct election of Senators by the people of each state, legislators from each state picked their two national Senators.

When the votes in the state legislature in Montana were counted, there were charges of bribery leveled at Clark and he failed in his attempt to be elected.

But Clark was undaunted, and he laid plans for the next election in 1899. This is a summary of what happened in that election contained in the book THE CLARKS, AN AMERICAN PHENOMENON: (pages 66-76)

> "Clark . . . had never yet entered a campaign without figuring what it would cost him. But once convinced that he had no chance to win except by spending, he prepared to pay a high price for the election [for the

elected office of senator] (in the Legislature.)

[The spokesman] for the committee [that had been appointed by the legislature to investigate rumors of bribery] announced that $30,000 had been offered to him and three other legislators by agents of William A. Clark as the price of their votes.

When the final ballot was taken, Clark had fifty-four votes. It was estimated that they had cost him four hundred and thirty one thousand dollars.

In December, 1899, [a Senator from Montana] presented in the United States Senate memorials petitioning the Senate to withhold the seat from Clark and to investigate the election and declare it void.

The committee . . . began an investigation on January 5, 1900 and continued it until April 6.

On April 10, 1900, the Committee unanimously voted to recommend that Clark's title to a seat in the Senate be declared void."

Clark resigned his seat and conspired with his son to get the Lieutenant Governor to appoint Clark to the vacancy his letter of resignation had created while the Governor was out of the state.

When the Governor returned, he revoked the Clark appointment and appointed someone else.

Clark immediately started his campaign for the next election in 1901, and on January 16 of that year, he was elected to the United States Senate.

That means that Jesse James, under the alias of William Andrews Clark, was elected to the Senate of the United States in 1901. He served for only one term, until 1907, but for six years, Jesse James, the famous outlaw, sat in the Senate of the United States.

But Clark's biggest payoff was yet to come.

During the economic crash of 1893, Augustus Heinze, one of the three "copper kings" mentioned in the book THE WAR OF THE COPPER KINGS said that Clark had:

> "succeeded in interesting the New York agents of Baring Brothers, the famous British bankers"

in building a copper smelter in Butte. The author continued:

> "The Barings were important men in the financial world, and had been for more than a century, second only to the Rothschilds as international bankers."

This was the first incursion of the European bankers into the Montana copper industry as far as I can determine, and it would later pay off handsomely for William Andrews Clark.

That led to the introduction of Standard Oil money into Montana, when Marcus Daly, another "copper king," merged his holdings with those of Standard Oil, owned primarily by the Rockefeller family, into the Amalgamated Copper Company. (Page 211 of THE WAR OF THE COPPER KINGS)

That book identifies the new owners of the Amalgamated:

> "Marcus Daly was to be president, **Henry H. Rogers**, vice-president, William G. Rockefeller, secretary-

treasurer; and James Stillman, J.P. Morgan and Governor Flower on the board of directors." (Page 214)

One must reconcile the previous comments I made about James/Clark/Dalton and his reluctance to become involved with business transactions where others might want to ask questions about his past. Yet, here Clark involved himself with some of the world's leading bankers and industrialists.

There is no way to know, but it seems as if he did not fear their asking probing questions because THEY KNEW HE WAS JESSE JAMES!

What other explanation makes sense?

These individuals certainly could have made his past public if they had discovered the truth .... yet there is not one public record of their having done so.

I will leave that to the reader to decide.

But back to the issue at hand.

William G. Rockefeller was one of the younger brothers of John D. Rockefeller, considered by many to be perhaps this nation's wealthiest man. In fact, the New York Times of September 29, 1975, called John D. Rockefeller this nation's first billionaire.

The primary source of the Rockefeller family fortune was oil, primarily through his oil company called Standard Oil, but with the purchases of William G., the Rockefeller family was moving into the copper industry in Montana.

The Rockefeller family's involvement in political conspiracy was best explained by historian Gary Allen in his book entitled THE ROCKEFELLER FILE:

"If there is one [family] dynasty that wants to rule the world, it is the Rockefellers."

It is not surprising then, to discover that Clark:

"sold out to the Amalgamated, [described as being the 'child of Standard Oil' on page 282 of THE WAR OF THE COPPER KINGS] turning over to the trust [decribed as "the Standard Oil Copper Trust" (page 290)] a large part of his most coveted property in Butte." (Page 241 COPPER KINGS)

The date he sold these interests to Standard Oil is not clear in this book, but it seems to be around 1901, the year he went to Washington D.C. as a U.S. Senator.

Whatever remaining assets that Clark had in the state of Montana, they were purchased "before the death of Senator Clark [1925]." So, whatever the Senator owned, it is quite likely Standard Oil now owned.

So the merger of Clark and Rockefeller was a good marriage: both had other interests than business!

This comment about the life of Senator Clark seems to confirm that he had something to hide:

"Clark stood alone, unique, in the fact that of all of the great enterprises with which he was connected, not one share of stock nor bond issue by any one of them was either listed or quoted or could be bought on any stock exchange in the United States."

A man with a hidden past was successfully hiding that past from the eyes of the inquiring stock or bond buyer.

And the reason seems to be obvious: Clark was protecting his secret identity of being Jesse James.

Perhaps a clue to Clark's personality can be taken from this comment made by Robert A. Pinkerton in the Richmond Democrat of November 20, 1879: THE ASSASSINATION OF JESSE JAMES by Ron Hansen, page 122:

> "I consider Jesse James the worst man, without exception, in America. He is utterly devoid of fear, and has no more compunction about cold-blooded murder than he has about eating his breakfast."

This view was shared by **Mark Twain**, (his real name was **Samuel L. Clemens**) the American writer and humorist, about a meeting he had with Senator Clark on January 28, 1907. This is what **Mr. Twain** wrote in his book entitled MARK TWAIN IN ERUPTION (pages71 and 72):

> "I [meaning the writer **Mark Twain**] am a person of elevated tone and of morals that can bear scrutiny, and am much above associating with animals of [Sen. William Andrews] Clark's breed.

> He is as rotten a human being as can be found anywhere under the flag; he is a shame to the nation, and no one has helped to send him to the Senate who did not know that his proper place was the penitentiary, with a chain and ball on his legs.

> To my mind, he is the most disgusting creature that the republic has produced since Tweed's time."

It can be inferred by that reference to "Tweed" that **Mr. Twain** was referring to "Boss" William Tweed. Mr. Yeatman in his book entitled FRANK AND JESSE (page101) wrote about Mr. Tweed:

> ". . . the New York Times was busy exposing 'Boss' William Tweed, head of the New York City Department of Public Works. Tweed had built a corrupt political machine based on kickbacks, fraudulent contracts, bribery, fake vouchers, and ghost employees.
>
> Some two hundred million dollars had been siphoned out of the municipal treasury over six years."

Twain's anecdote is interesting, one that partially confirms a story he told in another book, this one entitled MARK TWAIN AND I, page 1:

> "Some time ago I was making a purchase in a small town store in Missouri. A man walked in and, seeing me, came over with outstretched hand and said, 'You're **Mark Twain**, ain't you?'
>
> I nodded.
>
> 'Guess you and I are 'bout the greatest in our line,' he remarked.
>
> 'What is your name?' I inquired.
>
> 'Jesse James.'"

Neither of these stories reveal whether **Twain** knew that the Jesse James he met was in truth the Senator Clark he had written about before.

So it appears as if **Mark Twain** knew Jesse as Jesse and Clark as Clark.

The official story of William Andrews Clark ended on March 2, 1925, when the Senator "died of pneumonia" in New York City. According to the New York Times, the Senator was 86 years old, but to those who knew that Clark was an alias used by Jesse James, he was but 78 years of age. This discrepancy was another example of Jesse telling a lie so that those who knew him under the alias of William Andrews Clark would know that Jesse was still alive, and the New York Times reported the 86 year age of the deceased Senator. Of course, if he had been the real William Andrews Clark, he would have been 86 years of age in 1925.

But the truth of the story, as told by J. Frank Dalton, is that he "killed off" the Senator in 1925, because of the Senator's direct involvement in the "Teapot Done scandal" of the 1920's that had attempted to remove **Warren G. Harding** from the Presidency of the United States. Jesse was quoted as saying:

> "I've been involved in scandals before, but as Senator Clark I'm big potatoes. The government will really dig in this one and I could end up with a rope around my neck when they learn I'm Jesse James, wanted for murder on more than a few accounts."

To my knowledge, Dalton never revealed just what his involvement in the Teapot Dome Scandal was, but it is known that it involved oil interests seeking to discredit the **Harding** Administration. Apparently they were unsuccessful in removing the President, and it is possible they took another approach: **Warren G. Harding** got "blood poisoning" at a banquet and died on August 2, 1923 about 19 months before his term expired.

Perhaps the best one line statement about the character of President **Harding** was supplied by **Harry M. Daugherty**, his Attorney General, who wrote this in his book entitled THE INSIDE STORY OF THE HARDING TRAGEDY: (page 282)

"He wasn't a chum [friend] of any international banker."

Perhaps that explains why the Teapot Dome Scandal was created, and why the President got "food poisoning."

And why Senator Clark was so heavily involved in the scandal itself!

In any event, Dalton said that he went to Paris, France, after "dying of pneumonia," for a year to settle things down, before he returned to America.

Little is known, at least to this researcher, about the period of Clark's life between 1925 and 1948, when he surfaced in Lawton, Oklahoma.

But now the world can know a great deal more about the life of William Andrews Clark, the alias of Jesse James.

chapter twenty-three
THE 1995 EXHUMATION OF CHARLIE BIGELOW

Those who do not believe J. Frank Dalton's story are quick to offer the results of the exhumation of Jesse James' body in Kearney, Missouri between the months of July of 1995 and February of 1996 as proof that the real Jesse James has already been found, and that Dalton could therefore not be Jesse.

It might be of value to relate herein the story of this exhumation and the conclusion it reached that the "REAL" Jesse James was proven to have been buried in that cemetery in Kearney.

The story starts after the funeral of "Jesse" on April 6, 1882. The body of the outlaw was taken from the funeral parlor in St Joseph, Missouri, to Kearney, Missouri, where it was buried on the James farm, about 50 feet from the farmhouse occupied by Jesse's mother Zarelda.

The body stayed at the James farm until June 29, 1902 when it was removed to the Mt. Olivet Cemetery in Kearney, Missouri. It was reported at the time that the body was placed in a metal casket, and then re-buried in the cemetery.

When the exhumation of the body started on July 17, 1995, the diggers did not find the metal casket in the grave. They found a badly decomposed wooden one. This was of immediate concern to Dr. James E. Starrs, the man in charge of the exhumation process.

The Kearney Courier newspaper put out a special report on this exhumation procedure called PROBING and it reported on this problem. It quoted Dr. Starrs as saying:

> "We've been had. What we've found at this point is some bone in the midst of a wooden casket. If it was a metal casket [as reported by the papers at the time of the reburial] they were wrong."

It doesn't seem to be reasonable to conclude that those who were actually reporting on the reburial in 1902 were wrong when they reported seeing a metal casket and Dr. Starrs in 1995 was right when he found a wooden casket. It seems to stretch credulity to conclude that those who had actually watched the reburial would have made such a serious mistake as to report that a wooden casket was buried as a "metal casket."

It certainly is reasonable to conclude that mistakes could be made during the writing of newspaper articles, but this is a simple "either-or" issue: either the casket was metal or it was wood. And the reports of the time said it was "metal."

But Dr. Starrs apparently made no attempt to reconcile the two differing statements and the exhumation process continued.

The Dr. went on to say after the DNA results on the remains of the body were in:

> "I'll go out on the deep end . . . and say that I feel with a reasonable degree of scientific certainty that we have the remains of Jesse James."

Notice that the Dr. was not confident he had "certain" scientific proof that the body was that of Jesse James; he said that he "would go out on the deep end."

Dr. Starr made additional comments like this one:

> ". . . . everything we have that indicates a direct relationship to Jesse James indicates a consistency with everything we analyzed having come from Jesse James. And that's how far we can go and it's as far as I am willing to go.
>
> There is nothing to exclude and everything to include." (Yeatman, page 372)
>
> ". . . . everything that we have is consistent with the remains being those of Jesse James and I'm going to be locked in to the term 'consistent with.'" (Yeatman, page 372)

The Kearney newspaper article went on to explain, in part, why Dr. Starrs would only say "consistent with:"

> "Mitochondrial [mt] DNA extracted from one of Jesse's teeth matched the mtDNA taken from the blood of Robert Jackson. The Oklahoma City man is a descendent of a direct line of females from Jesse's sister, Susan. She and Jesse received the same mtDNA from their mother Zarelda. MtDNA can be passed on maternally."

What that means is that Jesse James, the male descendent of Zarelda James, could not have passed on Zarelda's DNA to his offspring, only the female children of Zarelda can.

So they could use the DNA of some offspring of Zarelda's

female descendants, in this case Jesse's sister Susan Lavenia James. So the exhumation team utilized the DNA provided by two direct descendants of Miss James, Robert Jackson, the grandson of Jesse's sister, and his nephew Mark Nikkel.

But there were those who were not satisfied with the process. One was:

> ". . . Bud Hardcastle, who said he heard about a discrepancy in what the exhumation team found last month. He heard that hair found in the grave was black, not Jesse's true brown.
>
> People involved in the exhumation brushed aside that comment: no hair of any color was found in the grave." (Page 12 THE KEARNEY COURIER PROBING A MYSTERY special collector's edition)

Notice that there was NO hair found in the casket by the exhumation team, yet they reported they had utilized some hair to draw some DNA conclusions.

The same article points out that Dr. Starrs asked the James Museum at the James farmhouse to supply them with some of the hair that the museum claimed came from the grave when it was re-entered in 1978 after the original body had been removed in 1902. Some of that hair was provided to Dr. Starrs and was tested by his staff and all that which had been provided was destroyed in the testing.

But it is fair to observe that no one knew for certain that this hair had come from the body originally buried in the James grave in 1882.

There are scientific reasons why hair located at another location cannot be used in scientific testing. The reason is simple: the scientists cannot verify that the sample is legitimate because they cannot certify that it came from the original site. In the case of the James exhumation, the fact that people say it was removed from the grave site of Jesse James would not be sufficient to utilize it in the DNA testing.

Scientists use the Latin phrase "in situ" when they remove materials from a site that they are studying. Those two words mean "in position, in its original place." That means that they will only state that certain items can be tested or exhibited if they know for certain that they were taken at the site where they were claimed to have been deposited.

That means that they will not use a bone brought into a museum by a lucky hiker who claims he found it at "site A" because they cannot say with certainty that it came from that site since they did not find it themselves and record its location scientifically. So for them to announce that it was found at "site A," they must have found it there themselves, preferably still in the ground or in the rock as a fossil. They must find it under scientific documentation at that site, meaning they would have to record that it was found "in situ" with some sort of evidence, such as a photograph of it at its original site, or other scientists certifying that they saw it at its original site.

These teeth and hair samples utilized in the James exhumation were not found "in situ" and therefore should not have been utilized in this scientific investigation. (In other words, they could not be certain that the hair or the teeth had come from the grave since they did not see it "in situ.")

In fact, Betty Duke, a James researcher, reported that:

"The hair used for testing was retrieved from the James Farm Museum. [This] museum has a sample of Zarelda James Samuel's [Jesse's recognized mother] hair on display."

If it was Zarelda's hair that Dr. Starrs used in the DNA testing process presuming that it had come from the grave of Jesse James, there are two major problems:

1. He obviously could not be certain that the hair was from the body inside the casket, and

2. If it was the hair of Zarelda James, they were testing her hair's DNA against the DNA of her own descendants.

Either way, that is not called SCIENCE!

And if the hair was the hair claimed to have come from the grave, the scientists could not use it either because it had not been found "in situ."

But in spite of all of these problems, Professor Starrs reported when he had concluded his investigation:

"I'll go out on the deep end . . . and say with a reasonable degree of scientific certainty that we have the remains of Jesse James."

The use of the phrase "I'll go out on the deep end" implies that the Professor DID NOT FIND THE SCIENTIFIC EVIDENCE that the body in the grave was the body of Jesse James. That's why he had to "go out on the deep end."

These are not the words of a scientist who has just scientifically proven that a body is the body of the victim because the DNA had matched. These are the words of a scientist who is using a "non-scientific" approach: "we think it is Jesse because the evidence appears to match."

The Kearney article continued:

"Other findings supported the case for Jesse:

Mitochondrial DNA: A match. MtDNA tests were done on several bones and teeth but only one tooth and head hair retrieved from the James Farm Museum carried sufficient mtDNA for testing. Test results from the hair still are being formulated."

Notice that the material taken from the James farm was used in the DNA testing, and that they were not removed from the casket or the grave site. Therefore any scientific research done on these items cannot give scientific results: in other words:

THE SCIENTISTS CANNOT SAY WITH ANY CERTAIN-TY THAT THE BODY BURIED AS JESSE WOODSON JAMES WAS INDEED THE BODY OF JESSE WOODSON JAMES, the son of Zarelda and Robert James.

Yet the Arizona Daily Star, my local morning newspaper, of October 29, 1995 (page A9) carried an article that read:

"DNA helps let Jesse James rest in peace."

But the article that accompanied the headline did little to convince the skeptic. It read, in part:

"Preliminary DNA tests concluded last month that scraps of bone and strands of hair exhumed from the grave [please re-read the comments made above about "the hair:" the scientists cannot say with certainty that they were exhumed from the grave] PROBABLY belonged to James." (Emphasis on PROBABLY by Epperson.)

So "uncertainty" and "probably" have replaced "scientific certainty."

So it is fair to conclude:

Jesse James DOES NOT rest in peace after the DNA testing.

But the media has convinced the American people that the issue has been settled .... once and for all.

But there is even more reason to believe the DNA tests have no scientific validity.

That information follows.

chapter twenty-four
JAMES SHOT BUT
NOT JAMES BURIED

One of the great mysteries of this entire exhumation in 1995 is the one regarding the DNA taken from a tooth supposedly coming from the body of Jesse James.

Let me try and describe the problem as briefly and as clearly as I can.

The St. Joseph Weekly Gazette of April 5th, 1882, the second day after the shooting, reported on an interview they had conducted with Zee James, the alleged wife of Jesse James, about the shooting. In that interview, they asked her this question:

> The Gazette:
> "Was Jesse a drinking man?"

> Her answer was:
> "No sir. He never drank, smoked nor chewed."

It must be remembered that the "official" story is that Zee had been married to Jesse for approximately 8 years prior to the shooting, so it can be reasonably concluded that a wife of 8 years would certainly know whether or not her husband "drank, smoked or chewed."

Now this poses a real problem, because of what the exhumers found in the casket dug up in the Kearney cemetery.

They removed a total of 14 teeth from the grave and presumed that they could use them for DNA testing. Experts know that the teeth are the last to decay in the grave and that they can be utilized as an excellent source of the DNA needed to draw some conclusions.

However, Dr. Mark Stoneking, the researcher doing the DNA tests, stated that these teeth were too heavily corroded and stained "showing that they belonged to a regular tobacco user."

There is only one conclusion one could draw from these two opposite statements, if the testimony of both parties is correct:

THE BODY EXHUMED
WAS NOT THAT OF
THE MAN MARRIED TO
ZEE JAMES,
THE ALLEGED WIFE OF JESSE JAMES

Since the bones of the deceased were too badly damaged from the moisture in the ground, and since the teeth were too badly damaged due to excessive tobacco use, the exhuming team needed to secure another source of the needed DNA.

This led the researchers back to the year of 1978, when Clay County, the county in which the James farm was located, purchased it to make it into a museum.

Milton "Milt" Perry, the manager of the farm at that time, dug into the former grave site and reportedly found two teeth. These teeth were placed in a tupperware container and later returned to the grave when he augured a hole into the grave site and returned them in the bowl into the ground.

Dr. Starrs apparently went to the courts seeking permission to exhume this site in an attempt to find the tupperware container. He reportedly found it but there were no teeth in it.

He must have heard that the James Farm Museum had two teeth that were claimed to have come from the grave site. It appears as if these were obtained for the DNA testing. It has not been made clear as to where these teeth came from.

They certainly could have been the two teeth reportedly taken from the grave site in 1978 but not returned in the tupperware bowl. They could have also come from Zarelda, or from any of the James family members, including Jesse himself. (Wouldn't that be ironic if the two teeth had come from the head of Zarelda James, and her DNA samples matched the DNA taken from her own family!) (Or even more ironic, that they came from the real Jesse Woodson James! That could mean that they tested Jesse Woodson James' own teeth to see if "Jesse James" was really Jesse Woodson James!)

According to Gene Gentrup, the Associate editor of the Kearney Courier:

> "Starrs said a tooth collected from the James Farm Museum provided the necessary mtDNA to prove with a reasonable certainty that the remains buried in Mr. Olivet Cemetery are indeed [those belonging to] Jesse James."

(It is possible that this singular "tooth" was one of the original two, meaning that the testers would have needed to only take the DNA from one tooth, so that the other one could be returned to the museum.)

Now, the same objection that was raised about the hair can be raised about these teeth (or one tooth) not being found "in situ."

Just who did these teeth belong to?

But no matter who they came from, they were not the teeth of the victim in the original Jesse James site in Kearney if Mrs. Jesse James was telling the truth about her husband who "never drank, smoked nor chewed." If the teeth at the James farm were from the body exhumed in the Kearney cemetery, they would have been too badly corroded from tobacco, and they were not. Obviously they were in good enough condition to be tested for DNA.

That means THE TOOTH DID NOT COME FROM THE JAMES BODY EXHUMED IN KEARNEY, MISSOURI!

Those teeth from the body were too badly corroded by tobacco.

That means they had to come from some other person, if Mrs. James was telling the truth about her husband.

Betty Duke reported in her review of the whole subject:

> "If the teeth from the Mt. Olivet site [the cemetery in Kearney, the site of the second burial of Jesse James] had yielded the mtDNA results that Starrs was banking on, he probably wouldn't have even considered using a tooth with a very questionable origin from a Tupperware bowl.
>
> And now that we know that the tooth was not in the bowl, one has to ask:

234

Just where did the teeth used for testing come from? Zee James has stated that they could not have come from her husband!"

But, since this book is attempting to show the nation that the man shot was not Jesse James, but Charlie Bigelow, there is no other conclusion than this one:

CHARLIE BIGELOW SHOT, BUT
NOT CHARLIE BIGELOW BURIED!

chapter twenty-five
THE EXHUMATION OF 2000

On May 30, 2000, the quiet, tranquil cemetery in Granbury, Texas was broken by the noise of members of the media and people who had come to see the exhumation of perhaps the cemetery's most famous resident: J. Frank Dalton.

Bud Hardcastle, the James researcher who had arranged for the exhumation on behalf of Jesse Quanah James and Charles A. James, two of Jesse's grandsons, was optimistic that once the body had been exhumed, DNA tests could determine once and for all if J. Frank Dalton was in truth the fabled Jesse Woodson James.

There is a family plot in the cemetery containing room for what appears to be six graves, outlined by a little 2" to 3" high concrete wall, and one of the grave sites inside this plot was the one that had a tombstone in front of it marked:

JESSE WOODSON JAMES
Sept. 5, 1847
Aug. 15, 1951
supposedly killed in 1882

and it was here that Mr. Hardcastle had permission to dig.

However, when the gravesite was opened, the hoped for "wooden casket" that Dalton was buried in was not found. Instead, a much larger metal "vault" containing a casket was in the grave and this posed a problem. The records showed that Dalton had been buried in a "wooden casket" yet none was to be found in the gravesite presumed to be his.

Permission to inspect the metal vault was obtained by the exhumation team and it was removed and taken to a second location where it could be opened. DNA samples were taken from the body in the casket inside this vault, but they proved that the body belonged to a family member of those who owned the burial plot and not that of J. Frank Dalton. The man in the vault was Henry Holland, (1907 - 1973,) a husband of one of the family members who owned the plot.

However, the fact that there was a metal vault instead of a wooden casket in the grave site proved to be a blessing in disguise.

The original plan of the exhumation was to dig down to the wooden casket, presumably in a state of deterioration, and then the necessary bone, teeth and hair samples could be removed for testing. The plan must have then been for the burial area to be filled in and then possibly the remaining material of that which had been removed for the testing, if there was any, could be replaced after it had served its purpose.

It does not appear as if it would have been necessary to have removed the wooden casket and the remains for the removal of only certain parts of the body.

Since the metal vault did not appear to match the details of the earlier burial of J. Frank Dalton, Mr. Hardcastle did not have permission to remove the vault.

However, since he had not located the original casket containing the body of Dalton, he sought permission to remove the vault and examine the contents of the casket it protected, and it was granted. It was determined that they would have to remove the vault so that they could open it.

They asked the diggers to remove the dirt around the vault so that they could place straps around it to pull it out of the ground, and that meant that they had to remove an extra foot or so on all sides of the vault. The dirt was removed and the straps placed around the vault and it was pulled out of the grave site.

But the fortunate thing that happened was that while they were digging the dirt from the left side of the vault, they discovered a wooden casket buried where no record exists of there having been a burial. This gravesite was not marked by a tombstone to identify it either. It was simply a grassy area to the left side of Dalton's alleged burial site.

It is conceivable that the Dalton tombstone was placed in front of another burial site. It is possible that those who buried Dalton in 1951 were attempting to protect his body from grave robbers and had placed the tombstone one site over to the right, to throw any diggers off, but details about the exact location of the grave of Dalton in this plot are sketchy.

As of this writing, September of 2000, permission is being obtained to dig up this casket to see if the remains there were those of Mr. Dalton. (That permission has still not been obtained as of October, 2005.)

So this chapter on the Jesse James story cannot be closed until the DNA tests are made and the results come in from the scientists. And that does not seem to be likely at the present.

And it appears as if someone does not want the casket opened of this unmarked grave site.

chapter twenty-six
DALTON AND CLARK

One of the evidences that J. Frank Dalton was in truth William Andrews Clark is the fact that both men were approximately the same height.

When I visited Jerome, Arizona to do some research for this book, I visited the offices of the Jerome Historical Society. They showed me a photograph of William Andrews Clark standing beside an automobile. There were no details as to when this photograph had been taken, nor what type of car he was standing by.

I was later able to discover that the vehicle was a 1913 Cadillac 4 door touring car, and through a current owner of one such vehicle, I was able to determine the height of that car. The owner told me he had had to build a special covered trailer to transport it from where he purchased it to his home in Wyoming. He told me that he had measured the car at 88 inches (7' 4" tall) high at the rear window.

Using this height at a given, I then measured the height of Sen. Clark against that constant.

And the Senator was approximately 5' 8" tall.

Several writers have commented on Clark's short stature. The following comments are found in the chapter entitled THE MAN FROM MONTANA, William Andrews Clark, in the book written by Herbert V. Young entitled GHOSTS OF CLEOPATRA HILL, MEN AND LEGENDS OF OLD JEROME [Arizona]:"

"The man was a small man physically . . . ."

"Though short of stature . . . ." and

"his lack of height . . . ."

William Daniel Mangam in his book THE CLARKS AN AMERICAN PHENOMENON made this statement about Clark's size:

"Years afterwards, Gus Graeter, one of the old timers of Bannack [Montana], was able to remember and to describe Clark as he appeared at that time. A LITTLE red haired man, Gus called him . . . ." (Emphasis by Epperson)

There are several comments made about how tall J. Frank Dalton was.

The Post Mortem conducted on the body of Mr. Dalton was done at Este's Funeral Home, in Granbury, Texas, on August 17, 1951. Present were the Sheriff of Hood County, the director of the Funeral Home, and four of Dalton's friends.

That report listed J. Frank Dalton at 5' 8 1/4" tall.

Rudy Turilli on page 29 of his book adds this additional evidence by Ola Everhard, Jesse's niece, about how tall J. Frank Dalton was. He reported:

"In 1939 a friend sent me a clipping from THE CORPUS CHRISTIE TIMES newspaper dated June 30, 1939. The caption [read] LAST OF **QUANTRILL**'S NOW LIVING IN CORPUS CHRISTI.

In the article Frank Dalton was said [to be] five feet eight and a half inches tall . . . ."

So both J. Frank Dalton and William Andrews Clark were approximately the same height: 5'8" tall.

chapter twenty-seven
JESSE, A SHORT MAN

The young Jesse James was also relatively short in height.

He was described by the authors Phillip W. Steele and George Warfel in their book entitled THE MANY FACES OF JESSE JAMES on page 74:

> "Family memories further describe Jesse James as being a relatively small person at five feet, nine inches in height."

Another author who commented on Jesse's size was Robertus Love in his book entitled THE RISE AND FALL OF JESSE JAMES (page 128) This statement was made about Jesse in 1873 when he was 25 years of age. It was made by an unnamed man, a farmer, who hosted the James gang after the train robbery near Adair, Iowa.

The farmer described the leader of the gang as being:

> "Five feet seven or eight inches tall, light hair, blue eyes, heavy sandy whiskers . . . ."

The author adds this comment:

> "That was a fairly accurate description of Jesse James. Jesse was not quite twenty-six at the time."

Even with these descriptions of the height of Jesse, history has recorded that the man that has been recorded as being Jesse James in 1882 was a little taller.

The body of the man found dead in the "James house" in St. Joseph was a few inches taller. This was discussed on page 348 of THE RISE AND FALL OF JESSE JAMES by author Robertus Love. He quoted the Kansas City Times newspaper of a day or two after the shooting:

> "Jesse James was about five feet eleven inches in height . . . ."

This estimate about how tall Jesse was must have come from James Little, a member of Jesse's gang. This is how he testified at the Coroner's Inquest in 1882:

> "Q: Were you acquainted with Jesse James?
> A: Yes, sir.
> Q: How long did you know him?
> A: Ten years.
> Q: Will you describe to us the appearance of Jesse James?
> A: He was a man about five feet eleven inches . . . ." DAILY GAZETTE, page 4

So here the observer is asked to believe that Jesse was about 5' 7" or 5' 8" tall when he was nearly 26, but 5' 11" when he was 36. That is a 3 to 4 inch growth in 10 years, all after a young man traditionally stops growing.

This paradox is completely consistent with the conclusion that the man shot as Jesse James was Charlie Bigelow and not Jesse James, especially if J. Frank Dalton was both Jesse James and William Andrews Clark. But the reporters of the day did not question the disparity and they reported that "Jesse James is dead." Yet all of the three principals in this story were around 5'8" tall. Only Charlie Bigelow was taller.

chapter twenty-eight
SIMILARITIES: CLARK, DALTON AND JAMES

There are some other similarities between Jesse James, William Andrews Clark, and J. Frank Dalton, and while these similarities are not conclusive enough to prove that they are the same individual, they do tend to lend credibility to a conclusion that these three individuals were connected.

1. Both Jesse James and William Andrews Clark had an interest in the violin or fiddle.

In the book entitled JESSE JAMES WAS ONE OF HIS NAMES, the two authors tell their readers:

> "The real Jesse W. James was an accomplished violin player and loved classical music." JJ WAS ONE OF HIS NAMES, page 129

William Andrews Clark played the violin and was instrumental in helping found the Butte, Montana symphony orchestra, in which he often played.

2. The book entitled JESSE JAMES WAS ONE OF HIS NAMES written by Jesse James III and Del Schrader, claims on page 275 that he was "a 33rd Degree Mason."

William Andrews Clark was also a high ranking member of the Masonic Lodge.

A Masonic book, actually 4 volumes in length, entitled 10,000 FAMOUS FREEMASONS says this under the heading of "WILLIAM ANDREWS CLARK, (1839 - 1925):"

"U.S. Senator from Montana, 1901 - 1907. He was grand master [the equivalent of the state wide President of the Masons in Montana] of the Grand Lodge of Montana in 1877."

That thought was repeated in THE CLARKS, AN AMERICAN PHENOMENON by William Daniel Mangam, for thirty years a general business agent to one of Clark's descendents, in this quotation from page 58:

"As early as 1865 Clark had joined the Masonic Lodge at Virginia City. He was elected to higher offices, and in 1877 became Grand Master of the Grand Lodge of Montana."

So both had an active life inside the Masonic Lodge.

3.   The Police Gazette, a magazine that followed and printed the stories about Jesse back in the late 1800's, had copies of the Pinkerton Detective Agencies reports going back as far as the year 1874.

These reports listed the physical marks on the man they knew as Jesse James that were caused by six bullet wounds and other injuries.

When Dalton passed away, someone requested a complete medical examination of his body including whatever x-rays they possessed. Their next issue of their magazine reported:

"Jesse James Alive in 1950."

They listed the following marks on the body of Dalton as evidence (meaning they found these marks were common to both James and Dalton:)

1. Rope burns on neck.
2. Evidence of severe burns on feet.
3. Bullet hole through left shoulder.
4. Bullet hole in lower belly.
5. Bullet scar under left knee.
6. Bullet scar under right eye.
7. Bullet hole along hairline of forehead.
8. End of index finger "chewed" off.

So the Police Gazette was convinced that Dalton was the real Jesse James, because his body contained the marks they believed were on the body of Jesse James, the real outlaw.

Another report on Dalton's injuries came from the Granbury, Texas Convention Bureau, in what appears to be a Press Release discussing three of Granbury's most famous inhabitants: **John Wilkes Booth**, J. Frank Dalton and Davy Crockett.

This is what they released on J. Frank Dalton:

> "Just before his death, James befriended Hood County Sheriff Oran Baker, the last sheriff to live in Granbury's old 1885 limestone jail.
>
> Baker spent long hours visiting with James, [meaning J. Frank Dalton] and he conducted a postmortem examination of James' [meaning J. Frank Dalton's] body.
>
> In 1966, Baker wrote a newspaper article saying that he found 32 bullet wounds on James' [Dalton's] body,

and a rope burn scar on James' [Dalton's] neck.

Baker also wrote that he believed that the man who died in Granbury in 1951 was in fact Jesse James."

4.   In the book entitled THE CLARKS AN AMERICAN PHENOMENON, the author makes this additional comment about Marcus Daly (Clark's major rival in the copper industry of Montana):

"Daly was mortally ill, and control of the Daly enterprises was now vested in the directors of the Amalgamated Copper Company, which had been formed in 1898.

H.H. Rogers and others in the Standard Oil Company [the oil company owned by the Rockefeller family] had become heavy stockholders in the Amalgamated . . . ." [page 78 of THE CLARKS]

"Within a month, he [Clark] had entered into a temporary compact with the Amalgamated . . . ." (but no other details were provided, so it is unknown just what form this compact took,) [page 79 of THE CLARKS]

Some additional details were added to this part of the story in the book JESSE JAMES WAS ONE OF HIS NAMES (page 128):

"Clark [meaning Dalton/James] finally sold his Anaconda [Montana] interests to Rockefeller."

So J. Frank Dalton was confirming the reports of William Andrews Clark that he, as Clark, had sold his interests to the

247

Rockefeller family.

5.   The William Andrews Clark biography states that
        Clark had fathered children with an Indian woman:

> "In his early days in the west, before he married, Sen-
> ator Clark had some children by an Indian women, al-
> though he never acknowledged nor provided for
> them." (page 89 THE CLARKS)

According to the book entitled JESSE JAMES WAS ONE OF
HIS NAMES, page 272,

> "In 1870, Jesse W. James wed Maggie (Redwing)
> Wabuska (sometimes spelled Matuska), a Sioux In-
> dian woman."

> "Sweet old Aunt Cora, the daughter of Jesse Woodson
> James and Maggie Wabuska, a Sioux Indian woman,
> was living in Nashville, Tennessee . . . ."

For confirmation of these comments, two pictures of Maggie
Matuska are found on page 64 of the book entitled JESSE
JAMES AND THE LOST CAUSE.

Another writer wrote about another connection between Jesse
James and an Indian woman. It appears as if this is a report
about the same situation but this one mentions both Jesse and
Frank and two Indian women. William A. Settle Jr. wrote
this: (page 167 of JESSE JAMES WAS HIS NAME.)

> "In 1939 it was claimed that there has long been a
> legend in the Devils Nest country of Northern Ne-
> braska that in 1869 [the report above says the year
> was 1870] Frank and Jesse James came to that area

and established a trading post among the Indians.

There, under the names of Frank and Jesse Chase, they met and married two beautiful Indian sisters, the daughters of Thomas Wabasha. In 1870 Jesse's Indian wife bore him a son, named Joe Jesse Chase. On July 4th, 1870, Frank and Jesse left for parts unknown."

And the Kearney Courier newspaper in their Special Collector's Edition on the exhumation of Jesse's body in 1995, apparently believed Mr. Settle's account and printed it as quoted above.

So this article implies that the Jesse James had indeed fathered Indian children "although he [too] never acknowledged nor provided for them" just like the Clark biography stated.

Each of these items by themselves do not constitute proof that Jesse James and William Andrews Clark were the same man, but they are additional evidence to all of the other evidence.

I believe that all of this evidence is that William Andrews Clark was Jesse Woodson James.

chapter twenty-nine
GRANMA CLARK

As part of the research for this book, I read a book on Jerome, Arizona, the location of the United Verde Mine that William Andrews Clark had owned for many years. I called one of the authors of this book to discuss her interest in the story of William Andrews Clark.

She told me that she was currently researching her own book on the Senator but was having difficulty in getting assistance from living members of the Clark family.

I asked her if she knew why that might be and she responded that she had no idea.

I informed her that it was possible that the reason was because the Senator was in truth the real Jesse James.

This would certainly explain why the Clark family would not wish to make the story of their famous relative known to the public since he had done all he could to keep it secret.

I have had similar experiences with getting the Clarks to assist in the telling the truth about Mr. Clark. And I would like to relay one story that confirms that many of their family members know that Senator William Andrews Clark was indeed the outlaw Jesse James

I am an historian/lecturer/writer who has written three other books on the subject of THE CONSPIRATORIAL VIEW OF HISTORY. I have chosen to self-publish my books because of their controversial nature.

I created the publishing company named PUBLIUS PRESS to market my books, and I sell them to individuals, book-stores and wholesalers.

I often get phone orders and one of these had an impact on my research into the story of Jesse James.

This particular call came from a gentleman who ordered one copy of one of my books, and as I was taking his name and address to send it to him, he told me his last name was Clark. This led to my questioning him if he had an ancestor named William Andrews Clark, and he stated that he did. I then asked him if this gentleman was the U.S. Senator, railroad and copper mine owner, and he confirmed that his relative was the same gentleman.

The next question was difficult to ask because I respected his family's privacy concerning their famous ancestor, but I asked it after obtaining Mr. Clark's approval:

> "You don't have to answer this question, but I would appreciate it if you would. Does your family know that William Andrews Clark is the famous outlaw Jesse James?"

He answered the question with ease when he said:

> "Yes, I know that Clark was Jesse James. In fact, that is common knowledge inside my family."

I must admit that this answer stunned me because he was the first in the Clark family to confirm that his ancestor was the outlaw Jesse James.

We continued our discussion for some time, over several

more phone conversations.

But the following episode is the one that had the most impact on my research into this story.

During one phone conversation with this gentleman, I heard a shriek from his end of the telephone. He put the phone down and walked away to another part of the house. When he returned he explained:

> "That was my wife. She was looking through a book on Jesse James and saw a picture of Zarelda James Samuel [the woman recognized by all Jesse James researchers as the real mother of Jesse Woodson James] for the first time.
>
> She shrieked because that was the same woman we in the Clark family recognize as Granma Clark, the mother of William Andrews Clark!"

We discussed his wife's response a little further.

I informed him that there was a way we could confirm if they were the same woman. I told him that Zarelda James Samuel had lost part of her right arm in an explosion in her home that had also killed her son. This was the famous Pinkerton Detective's attempt to flush out Jesse and Frank James from inside their home.

It didn't work, and many historians believe that the two James brothers were not in the home that night.

The Clark on the phone reported that Granma Clark had lost part of her right arm as well as her son in an accident sometime in the past.

I think one can see the incredible chances that both of these women could look alike and also would have a similar story and not be the same person.

1.   Claims were made that they both were the mother of Jesse James and William Andrews Clark.

2.   They both lost a RIGHT arm in an accident.

3.   They both lost a son in the same accident.

4.   They looked so much alike that an observer would have to conclude they were the same woman.

The chances of these women not being the same woman are certainly beyond the possibilities of coincidence.

During one other conversation, he reported that his family would not be interested in assisting me develop the story of the Jesse James/William Andrews Clark connection, and I respectfully, and regretfully, accepted his statement.

I must admit in conclusion that this Clark family member and I have lost contact with each other since this conversation. So I have no way of checking to see if he has changed his mind.

All I can do now is tell the story as it occurred and then ask the reader to make up his own mind on the truthfulness of the caller's comments.

chapter thirty
HOW DID HE GET AWAY WITH IT?

In his book entitled THE RISE AND FALL OF JESSE JAMES, the author Robertus Love asks the final question about Jesse and his brother Frank: (Page 7)

"The Jameses, [meaning Jesse and Frank James] lasting sixteen years, established a world's record in the matter of keeping out of the law's clutches.

How was it possible?

Why was it permitted?"

The easy answer to this question is that the people of Missouri were afraid of Jesse and his gang. One author addressed that directly when he wrote:

". . . all Missouri was in terror of what would happen to anyone who gave information on the Jameses." (BREIHAN, page 110 of THE DAY JESSE JAMES WAS KILLED)

But Mr. Love pointed out that he believed there was a concealed, hidden answer as to why the James brothers were never captured. He wrote:

"Just why the sheriffs of hundreds of counties in a dozen states, the police forces of scores of cities and thousands of towns, the wide spreading detective nets of Allan and William Pinkerton, and all of the other man-hunting agencies failed to catch or kill these two outlawed brothers, although during the sixteen years from 1866 to 1882 the avid sleuths were on the trail almost constantly, will develop as this narrative [meaning Mr. Love's book, page 8] proceeds."

Mr. Love then urges his readers to find the reason himself, but that he will provide him with clues as he reads his book. This is how he put it:

"The wise peruser [reader] will read between the lines, where frequently the marrow of the matter inheres [resides.]" (page 8)

This author was telling his readers that the reason that Jesse and his brother were able to survive all of the bandit years lies concealed in the words of his book. According to him, the wise reader will have to figure this out for themselves.

But Mr. Love does provide his reader a clue on page 285 when he talks about Jim Cummings, a reported gang member:

". . . Jim, being of the brotherhood, would remain silent like the others."

Since Jesse James was a member of the Masonic Lodge, and they sometimes refer to themselves as a Brotherhood, it could be inferred that Mr. Love was referring to the Masonic fraternity as "the brotherhood" because it is known that one Masonic brother will not reveal secrets about another Masonic brother, especially if that brother is in some sort of difficulty.

To prove this, one has only to go to the Masonic literature.

This requirement that the brothers remain silent about matters concerning their brothers is found in the OBLIGATIONS portion of their rituals that a Mason goes through as he progresses towards becoming a higher ranking member of the lodge.

The first instance of this occurs in the 12th Degree Ritual, (it might be remembered that the Masons have 32 Degrees, with an honorary 33rd Degree being the last one) when the initiate is told he can expect assistance from his brother Masons:

> "I, (name) do most solemnly and sincerely promise and swear, binding myself under the penalty of being deserted and abandoned by my friends and denounced and hunted down by my enemies and of forfeiting all claim to assistance in danger, comfort in calamity and SUPPORT IN DIFFICULTY FROM ANY MASON IN THE WORLD, if I should be guilty of wilfully and intentionally violating this my solemn obligation of a Grand Master Architect [the title of the 12th Degree.] . . .." MAGNUM OPUS, 12th Degree, page 7

The Mason just swore that he would lose "THE SUPPORT OF ANY OTHER MASON . . . [if] IN DIFFICULTY" if he broke the vow of unwillingness to assist a brother. That means that all Masons are obligated to assist their fellow Masons if their fellow Masons were "IN DIFFICULTY."

Then it is further explained in the 14th Degree Ritual, that the initiate himself will assist his brothers in the Lodge, when he takes the following oath:

> "I furthermore promise and swear . . . that I will rescue them from danger . . . ." (Magnum Opus, 14th Degree, page 8)

256

Then the 15th Degree adds:

> "I furthermore promise and swear that I will assist, protect and defend my brethren of this degree by all lawful means consistent with the character of a true Mason . . . ." 15th Degree, MAGNUM OPUS page 10

The 16th Degree further extends the initiate's obligations:

> "I furthermore promise and swear that I will never abandon a Brother, in whatever adversity he may be, in combat, or in sickness, or in prison; but I will aid him with my counsel, my friends, my sword and my purse." MAGNUM OPUS, 16th Degree, page 7

The 17th Degree:

> "I furthermore promise and swear . . . that I will, at all times, when he has justice on his side, be ready to aid and support him against any who seek his life, or to destroy his honour, reputation, peace of mind or estate." MAGNUM OPUS, 17th Degree, page 8

The critic would be quick to point out, I am certain, that this obligation says that the brother Mason will defend his brother "when he has justice on his side." That certainly would not seem to apply when that brother needing the protection is Jesse James. And this author will concede that this obligation does indeed say that, but I hasten to remind the critic of the obligation that follows.

The 29th Degree has another obligation:

> "I furthermore promise and swear . . . that I will aid and assist, cherish and protect a worthy Brother

257

Knight, and see that no wrong be done him, if it be in my power to prevent it."

Notice here that there is no requirement to afford assistance but only "when he has justice on his side." That means that this higher obligation removes that condition. Here the helpful brother has no such obligation: just assist him no matter what the conditions are.

So the missing ingredient in the Jesse James story is the Masonic Lodge. The Masons around Jesse James, 33rd Degree Mason, constantly sought to assist him so as to not bring disfavor upon the reputation of the Masonic Lodge.

Because their obligations require them to do so.

And it worked.

The Jesse James story is now nearly complete: Jesse James was allowed to continue his work because his fellow Masons took oaths to protect him

Jesse James, outlaw, 33rd Degree Mason.

Jesse James, U.S. Senator, High Ranking Mason

Jesse James, copper magnate, High Ranking Mason

Jesse James, railroad tycoon, High Ranking Mason

And the 33rd Degree is the highest one in the Scottish Rite.

And it is honorary, meaning the Mason must be invited in.

And Jesse James was invited in!

chapter thirty-one
"NOT A MATCH"

Technology has certainly progressed since the days of Jesse James. And I became aware of a modern technology called FORENSIC ANTHROPOLOGY in the year 2000.

The term is defined as:

"FORENSIC ANTHROPOLOGY: the identification of the cause of death of skeletal remains. In addition, the forensic anthropologist can determine the gender, approximate age, physical stature, and likely racial affiliation of the person in life."

Another service they can provide is the examination of the skeletal remains with a photograph of the individual in question, if one is in their possession, to see if the deceased individual is the one in the photograph.

I was hoping after I first heard about this that the field could be broad enough to determine if the photographs of the three men, James, Clark and Dalton, were of the same individual.

So I contacted the University of Arizona here in Tucson, because they have a department such as this and I learned that the nationally recognized authority teaching in this field had retired. I got in touch with him at home and he stated that he could not assist because he no longer had access to the laboratory at the university.

But he suggested that I contact his "best student" who he had trained at the University, who had graduated with a PhD and was then employed in that department at a major college in the Mid West (I have chosen not to reveal the names of either of these gentlemen, because I just don't think it is necessary.)

I corresponded with him over the internet originally, but we then had several phone conversations. This second professor was interested and I supplied him with the photographs of all three men that I had accumulated in my research.

After several months of time, in the year 2000, he called me back and stated that it was his opinion and that of his students in his classes who looked into the question as part of a class project, that:

"THERE WAS NO MATCH"

between James and Clark, and Clark and Dalton.

However, when I expressed my dismay at his conclusion, because of all of the other evidence that they were the same person, he stated:

**"HOWEVER, WE DO NOT HAVE
AN EXPERTISE IN DETERMINING
IF THE INDIVIDUALS ARE THE SAME
WHEN THERE ARE AGE DIFFERENCES."**

That means that their expertise lies in discovering whether skeletal remains are those of a known individual with a photographic history. They simply do not have the expertise in dealing with comparing two pictures to see if they are the same person, if there are age differences between the two individuals in the pictures.

And there are major age differences in this story: the James pictures ended in 1882, when Jesse was 35, the Clark pictures ended in 1925, when he would have been 78 and the Dalton pictures ended in 1951 when he was 103.

He explained that this was a field that needed research and he suggested that they might study the aging characteristics of someone like President Ronald Reagan because of the great number of photographs taken of him throughout his long life and his habits of keeping slim and in good physical condition.

So when he expressed the opinion of there was not a match between these three individuals, I was in a quandary.

After 30 some years of research into this story, plus knowledge of the research done by many others in the field who agreed with my assessment that Dalton was both Clark and James, I was at a loss to explain how modern science could not agree with all of that research.

And the only conclusion I could draw was that I had asked the wrong branch of modern science to do research in a field that they are not prepared to investigate.

And I do not know of a field of science I could ask for the final opinion.

I think it would be appropriate to go back to the years of 1948 to 1951, when people had a chance to determine if Dalton was really Jesse James, because Dalton had made his story available to the public and hundreds of people went to meet with him, in person.

I would like to quote from a series of 41 SWORN STATEMENTS cited in the back of the book entitled JESSE JAMES WAS ONE OF HIS NAMES. These were people who testified that J. Frank Dalton was the real Jesse Woodson James, after meeting with him in person:

"He is the real Jesse W. James all right. I would know him anywhere."

"My father was a Confederate veteran who knew Jesse W. James in West Texas, after he was supposed to have been killed in Missouri."

"I positively identify this man as Jesse James who once stayed with us for more than 11 months near Mooringsport along the Texas - Louisiana border."

"After talking to him about happenings of the past, I'm sure this man is Jesse W. James."

"I am convinced after talking with him he is the real JWJ [Jesse Woodson James.]"

"I knew Frank and Jesse James as a youth, I swear this white-bearded old gunman to be Jesse W. James."

"We [the statement of three witnesses] are convinced this man is Jesse W. James."

"This is the same man who visited us in Lufkin, Texas when I was 10."

"I believe this old man to be Jesse James."

"I am convinced he is the real Jesse W. James."

"The way he answered all the questions I put to him, some of them back to 1864, caused me to firmly believe he is the real

Jesse James."

"When I went to see him he knew me at once and he answered all my questions. It's him."

"I have never forgotten him, nor could I mistake anyone else for him now."

"Long after Jesse W. James was presumed killed in St. Joseph, Mo., in 1882, he came to see and visit my daddy almost every summer."

"I personally know he is JWJ [Jesse Woodson James.]"

"It was the real Jesse W. James who revealed himself in Lawton, Okla., in May, 1948."

"Jesse W. James visited my Nashville, Tenn., home in September, 1948. I most certainly knew and [had] every reason to know the famous old Jesse W. James. He was a friend of mine and my family for many years."

"J. Frank Dalton is Jesse W. James."

"The very first money I ever got was from Jesse James, back in about 1896, 14 years after he was supposedly killed in Missouri, but I'd know him anywhere."

"The actual and long-missing Jesse W. James died in Granbury, Texas, August 15, 1951."

"When I lived in New Mexico I knew Jesse W. James, long after [he was] supposed to be killed."

"Jesse didn't die in St. Joseph. He was alive and kicking

many, many years after that. He died in Texas in 1951."

"Jesse W. James died in Granbury, Texas, in 1951."

"He was the real Jesse W. James."

So there were many eye witnesses who actually met with Dalton and they were encouraged to probe the man's memory, and many of them confirmed that he was who he claimed to be, because they remembered details that only the real Jesse Woodson James would know, even those that were many years ago.

I still cannot explain why the FORENSIC ANTHROPOLO- GISTS claimed that "THERE WAS NO MATCH."

Because all of my research, plus the research of many others, all say:

"THERE IS A MATCH."

But I am willing to consider a compromise:

If the man called J. Frank Dalton WAS NOT Jesse Woodson James, but was able to convince many who actually knew the real Jesse James, who was he?

And how did he fool so many?

And the only explanation I can offer if he was not, is this one:

Possibly Mr. Dalton was a "double" for the real James. And that he had assumed that position during a great deal of the real James' life, from 1882 until his death sometime after 1925 and before 1948.

But this would require that the real Jesse told Mr. Dalton details of his very early childhood all the way from age 7 or 8 to possibly when he was in his 30's, before Dalton was "hired" to be his double.

Think about how difficult it would be for Dalton to remember all of the personal stories told to him by the real Jesse James if Dalton was a double.

This one, for instance:

"This is the same man who visited us in Lufkin, Texas when I was 10."

If this person was now an adult, that would mean that 20 to 30 years or more had passed since this event took place. How could Jesse have taught Dalton about this encounter? James might have forgotten it himself!

But the person said that Dalton remembered it. The only explanation that makes sense is that Dalton was the real James and this was a recollection of the real person.

Then Dalton would have had to live with the real James as James lived his life, including his days as an outlaw, a Senator, a railroad magnate, and as a "copper king."

However, there is NOT ONE shred of evidence that I have found in all of my years of research that ANYONE who looked into this story has ever claimed that there was a "mysterious man around Jesse who looked enough like him to be his double. And he was everywhere James was."

So it seems to be too much to presume that Dalton was just such a "look-alike." That means to me that there is ONLY

ONE POSSIBLE EXPLANATION:

JESSE JAMES
WAS BOTH
WILLIAM ANDREWS CLARK,
AND
J. FRANK DALTON.

To me, it is abundantly clear and the reason for that is that the evidence for that conclusion is abundant.

But I leave the final decision in your hands.

A FINAL THOUGHT

In the book entitled JESSE JAMES WAS ONE OF HIS NAMES, the two authors quote J. Frank Dalton as saying:

"The historians still haven't got it right."

Dalton was even more critical of histories on the West.

"Maybe someday somebody will come along and set the record straight."

This is my humble attempt at doing just that, at least in the matter of the true story of Jesse James.

I hope that history will judge my effort with some degree of fairness and acceptance..

My research has concluded that it is true:

Jesse James was a major player in America's past.

Jesse James, U.S. Senator.

BIBLIOGRAPHY

These are some of the books that I read to complete this book.

I am certain that one could argue that this list is not exhaustive, but the reader will notice that I have read the major works of those who believe in the "Jesse was killed in 1882" theory, as well as those written by those who believe that J. Frank Dalton was Jesse James.

Those works are:

ALBERT PIKE, THE MAN BEYOND THE MONUMENT, by James T. Tresner II, published by M. Evans and Company, New York. Copyrighted in 1995 by the Supreme Council 33rd Degree of the Southern Jurisdiction of the Scottish Rite, Washington D.C.

THE ASSASSINATION OF JESSE JAMES, by Ron Hansen, published by Harper Perennial, 1983

THE CLARKS, AN AMERICAN PHENOMENON, by William Daniel Mangam, published by Silver Bow Press, New York, 1939

THE COMPLETE AND AUTHENTIC LIFE OF JESSE JAMES, by Carl W. Breihan, published by Frederick Fell, Inc., New York, date of publication not shown

COW BY THE TAIL, by Jesse James Benton, published by Houghton Mifflin Company, Boston, 1943

THE CRITTENDEN MEMOIRS, compiled by Henry Huston

Crittenden, published by G.P. Putnam's Sons, New York, 1936

THE DAILY GAZETTE, St. Joseph, Missouri, Wednesday, April 5, 1882 edition

THE DAY JESSE JAMES WAS KILLED, by Carl Breihan, published by Frederick Fell, Inc., Publishers, New York, date of publication not shown

FRANK AND JESSE JAMES, by Ted P. Yeatman, published by Cumberland House, Nashville, 2000

THE GOLD RING, by Kenneth D. Ackerman, published in 1988 by Harper Business

A HISTORIC RESOURCE SURVEY OF CLARKDALE, ARIZONA, prepared for the town of Clarkdale, Arizona, 1989

IN THE SHADOW OF JESSE JAMES, by Stella F. James, published by The Revolver Press, 1990

JEROME AND THE VERDE VALLEY, by 8 authors, published by Thorne Enterprises, Sedona, Arizona, 1990

JEROME, A STORY OF MINES, MEN AND MONEY, no author shown, published by the Southwestern Monuments Association, no date of publication shown

JESSE AND FRANK JAMES, THE FAMILY HISTORY, by Phillip W. Steele, published by Pelican Publishing Company, 1987

JESSE JAMES AND THE LOST CAUSE, by Jesse Lee

James, published by Pageant Press, New York, 1961

JESSE JAMES, THE MAN AND THE MYTH, by Marley Brant, published by Berkley Books, New York, 1998

JESSE JAMES RIDES AGAIN, by Frank O. Hall and Lindsey H. Whitten, published by LaHoma Publishing Company, Lawton, Oklahoma, date of publication not shown

JESSE JAMES: RIDING HELL-BENT FOR LEATHER INTO LEGEND, by Joseph Geringer, published by Dark Horse Entertainment Inc., in 2000. Available on the internet by a free download at:
        www.crimelibrary.com/americana/jesse/author.htm

JESSE JAMES -- THE OUTLAW, by Henry J. Walker, published by Wallace-Homestead Co. of Des Moines, Iowa, 1961

JESSE JAMES WAS HIS NAME, by William A. Settle, Jr., published by the University of Missouri Press, Columbia, Missouri, 1966

JESSE JAMES WAS ONE OF HIS NAMES, by Del Schrader with Jesse James III, published by Santa Anita Press, Arcadia, California, 1975

LAS VEGAS, AS IT BEGAN -- AS IT GREW, by Stanley W. Paher, published by Nevada Publications, Las Vegas, 1971

THE LIFE AND TRAGIC DEATH OF JESSE JAMES, written by anonymous, published by Barclay & Co., Philadelphia, 1883

THE LIFE, TIMES & TREACHEROUS DEATH OF JESSE

JAMES, by Frank Triplett, published by Konecky & Konecky, New York, 1970

THE MANY FACES OF JESSE JAMES, by Phillip W. Steele, published by Pelican Publishing Co., 1995

MY JESSE JAMES STORY, by Joe Wood, published by Missourian Publishing Co., Washington, Missouri, 1989

THE RISE AND FALL OF JESSE JAMES, by Robertus Love, published by the University of Nebraska Press, Lincoln, 1925

ROBBER AND HERO, THE STORY OF THE NORTH-FIELD BANK RAID, by George Huntington, published by the Northfield Historical Society Press, Northfield, Minnesota, 1994

THEY CAME TO JEROME by Herbert V. Young, published by the Jerome Historical Society, Jerome, Arizona, 1972

THE TRUTH ABOUT JESSE JAMES, by Rudy Turilli, self-published by author, 1967

THE WAR OF THE COPPER KINGS, by C.B. Glasscock, published by the Bobbs-Merrill Company, of New York, date of publication not shown

THE WILLIAM A. CLARK COLLECTION, TREASURES OF A COPPER KING, a publication of The Corcoran Gallery of Art, Washington D.C., 1989

INDEX

--end of index--